英語通訳ガイドの基礎知識

著　西田一弘

ふくろう出版

はじめに

　通訳案内士試験は、日本語を話すことができない外国の観光客に付き添い、日本の文化・地理・歴史などの日本事情を紹介する「通訳案内士」を養成するための唯一の英語国家試験です。試験は英語・日本事情全般に関する1次試験（筆記試験）と英会話力と人物考査に関する2次試験（口述試験）があり、高度な語学力及び日本事情全般の広範囲な知識が問われます。

　通訳案内士試験に合格するには、高度の英語力のみならず、日本文化に精通することが必要です。その中でも難関と言われている、通訳案内士試験の英語1次試験や2次試験の合格に必要である「日本文化の知識を含めた英語力の養成」を行うことが本書の目的です。つまり、「通訳案内士」に必要な、「日本の文化の知識と、高度な英語力」を兼ね備えた国際的な日本文化コミュニケータの養成を目指します。英語のスピーキング力やライティング力が重要であることはもちろん、文書・口頭ともに日本事情を英語で説明するには、専門用語の知識と日本事象の知識に裏付けられた英語による説明能力が必要です。この知識と能力の獲得が、唯一の英語国家試験「通訳案内士試験」の一次試験（英語筆記試験）・二次試験（英語口頭試問）の合格に必要な「高度な英語力」獲得につながります。

　本書を使用して、その基礎となる日本文化の知識を兼ねそなえた英語力養成を目指しましょう。さあ、英語による日本文化コミュニケータを目指して、頑張りましょう。

映像教材

下記 URL から YouTube の映像教材で、**第 7 章 "JAPANESE CULTURE"** を勉強しましょう！
Kazuhiro Nishida & Giulia Barbieri

I https://youtu.be/yoSyEQmQZLM
II https://youtu.be/ckOYjB_hBfE
III https://youtu.be/r78s38my9b0
IV https://youtu.be/bW7pTUrI46g
V https://youtu.be/ZR27Jp8xveA
VI https://youtu.be/cvCev6cJgkY

「第1章 英文解釈 ―精読―」では、英文をどのように読んでいけば良いのかを、じっくり学習しましょう。「考えるべき事柄」と「その解答」をセットで述べる形式で進んでいます。

「第2章 日本事象・日本地理・日本史の理解」では、問題形式で日本事情、日本地理、日本史の知識を英語でどのように表現するのか、学習しましょう。

「第3章 英文解釈 ―多読・速読―」では、多読・速読に必要な内容を学習しましょう。「考えるべき事柄」と「その解答」をセットで述べる形式で進んでいます。

「第4章　日本史（応用）の理解」では、第2章の日本史の理解からさらに深い内容で、日本史の知識を英語でどのように表現するのか、学習しましょう。

　「第5章　英作文　―条件英作文―」では、英作文をする上で重要な内容を学習しましょう。「考えるべき事柄」と「その解答」をセットで述べる形式で進んでいます。

　「第6章　日本事情　―英単語 & 英文説明―」では、日本の文化を紹介する上で、重要な英単語と英文を学習しましょう。

　「第7章　JAPANESE CULTURE（実践演習）」では、日本文化を英文として、実際に紹介していきましょう。さらに、英単語、英文法、英作文の学習も行いましょう。

目 次

はじめに *1*
目次 *4*

第1章　英文解釈　―精読―   *5*

第2章　日本事象・日本地理・日本史の理解   *14*
問題1．≪日本文化事象≫ *14*
問題2．≪地理≫ *25*
問題3．≪歴史文化≫ *29*

第3章　英文解釈　―多読・速読―   *38*

第4章　日本史（応用）の理解   *51*
問題．　≪歴史応用≫ *51*

第5章　英作文　―条件英作文―   *78*

第6章　日本事情　―英単語 & 英文説明―   *90*

第7章　JAPANESE CULTURE（実践演習）   *97*
Ⅰ．The Japanese Climate *97*
Ⅱ．Japanese Religion *102*
Ⅲ．Bushido (The Way of Bushi) *108*
Ⅳ．Promotion According to Age vs. Ability *113*
Ⅴ．Japanese Annual Events *119*
Ⅵ．Japanese Tourism *125*

あとがき *131*

第1章

英文解釈 —精読—

「第1章 英文解釈 —精読—」では、英文をどのように読んでいけば良いのかを、じっくり学習しましょう。「考えるべき事柄」と「その解答」をセットで述べる形式で進んでいます。

問題：次の英文の下線部を和訳しなさい。

Kabuki is one of the three major classical theaters of Japan, together with the *No* and the *Bunraku* puppet theater. <u>*Kabuki* started in the early 17th century as a sort of variety show performed by troupes of itinerant entertainers. By the Genroku period, it had attained its first flourishing as a mature theater, and it continued, through much of the Edo era, to be the most popular form of stage entertainment. *Kabuki* reached its artistic peak with the magnificent plays of Tsuruya Namboku IV and Kawatake Mokuami.</u>

・スキミング（飛ばし読み―大意をつかむ―）の仕方は？

5 W 1 H：Who（・Whom）, When, Where, What, Why, How
　　　　　　　　①　　　　　②　　　③　　　④　　⑤　　⑥

<u>*Kabuki*</u> started in the <u>early 17th century</u> as a sort of variety
　④　　　　　　　　　　　②

show <u>performed</u> by troupes of itinerant <u>entertainers</u>. By the
　　　⑥　　　　　　　　　　　　　　　　①

5

Genroku period, it had attained its first flourishing as a
  ②
mature theater, and it continued, through much of the Edo era,
 ④   ②
to be the most popular form of stage entertainment.　*Kabuki*
   ⑥
reached its artistic peak with the magnificent plays of
  ⑥
Tsuruya Namboku IV and Kawatake Mokuami.

・スキミング（飛ばし読み―大意をつかむ―）の仕方は？
5 W 1 H：Who（-Whom）, When, Where, What, Why, How
      ①   ② ③ ④ ⑤ ⑥
④*Kabuki* 歌舞伎は，②early 17th century 17世紀の初め，⑥performed 行われて(過去分詞)，①entertainers 芸人，②Genroku era 元禄時代，④mature theater 円熟した劇，②Edo era 江戸時代，⑥the most popular 最も人気のある，⑥reached its artistic peak 芸術的な絶頂に達した

・紛らわしい文法事項

　Kabuki started in the early 17th century as a sort of variety show performed by troupes of itinerant entertainers.　By the Genroku period, it had attained its first flourishing as a mature theater, and it continued, through much of the Edo era, to be the most popular form of stage entertainment.　*Kabuki* reached its artistic peak with the magnificent plays of Tsuruya Namboku IV and Kawatake Mokuami.

第1章　英文解釈　―精読―

1. **過去形**（-ed：〜した）なのか
   過去分詞（-ed：〜されて）なのか
2. **現在分詞**（-ing：〜していて）なのか
   動名詞（-ing：〜すること）なのか
3. **It** の示すものは何か
   ①もの（具体的には何か）なのか
   ②不定詞（ **to 動詞**： 〜すること）なのか
4. **and** の働きは何か
   何と何を結びつけているのか
   ①文（S+V…）と文（S+V…）を結び付けているのか
   ②単語と単語を結びつけているのか（a, b, c, …**and** z）
5. **that** は何か
   ①指示語（それ、その、…）なのか
   ②接続詞（〜ということ）なのか
   ③関係代名詞、関係副詞（訳はない）なのか

・**紛らわしい文法事項**

　Kabuki started in the early 17th century as a sort of variety show performed by troupes of itinerant entertainers.　By the Genroku period, **it** had attained **its** first flourishing as a mature theater, **and it** continued, through much of the Edo era, to be the most popular form of stage entertainment.　*Kabuki* reached **its** artistic peak with the magnificient plays of Tsuruya Namboku IV **and** Kawatake Mokuami.

1. **過去形**（-ed：〜した）なのか　　　started, continued, reached,
   過去分詞（-ed：〜されて）なのか　　　　《performed》,
   　　　　　　　　　　　　　　　　　　had 《attained》
   　　　　　　　　　　　　　　　　　　（過去完了形）

7

2. 現在分詞（-ing：～していて）なのか　　　（a <u>dancing</u> girl）
   動名詞（-ing：～すること）なのか　　　　　flourishing
3. It の示すものは何か？
   ①もの（具体的には何か）なのか　　　　　it / its = kabuki
   ②不定詞（to 動詞：　～すること）なのか（It is good <u>to study</u>.）
4. and の働きは何か
   何と何を結びつけているのか
   ①文（S＋V…）と文（S＋V…）を結び付けているのか
   　　　　　　　　　　　　　　　　　　　　and it continued
   ②単語と単語をむすびつけているのか（a, b, c, …and z）
   　　　　　　　Tsuruya Namboku IV **and** Kawatake Mokuami.
5. that は何か
   ①指示語（それ、その…）なのか
   ②接続詞（～ということ）なのか
   ③関係代名詞、関係副詞（訳はない）なのか

・**英文読解のこつ**
1. 主語（S）、述語動詞（V）を見つける。
   接続詞、関係代名詞、関係副詞が入ると
   文（S＋V…）が1つ増えることになる。
2. 各単語の品詞（名詞、形容詞、動詞、副詞）を見極める。
   単語の意味がわからなくても品詞がわかれば
   文脈から単語の意味を類推できる。
3. 修飾語（形容詞句・節と副詞句・節）を見抜く。
   修飾語は（　）でくくり主語（S）、述語動詞（V）を見つけやすくする。
4. 代名詞（it, they …）が何を表わしているのかを見極める。
   原則は一番近くにある名詞である。

第1章 英文解釈 ―精読―

・品詞の分類
1. 人・事物の名称に関する語：＿＿＿＿、＿＿＿＿＿
2. 人・事物などの動作・状態に関する語：＿＿＿＿、＿＿＿
3. その他：接続詞、冠詞、前置詞、代名詞

・品詞の分類
1. 人・事物の名称に関する語：**名詞、形容詞**
2. 人・事物などの動作・状態に関する語：**動詞、副詞**
3. その他：接続詞、冠詞、前置詞、代名詞

・品詞の相互関係

　　四大品詞

　　＿＿＿＿詞　＋　＿＿＿＿詞　　She is a beautiful lady.
　　＿＿＿＿詞　＋　＿＿＿＿詞　　I will study hard.

　＊　単語の順序も表しているので注意。

・品詞の相互関係

　　四大品詞

　　形容詞　＋　名詞　　She is a beautiful lady.
　　動　詞　＋　副詞　　I will study hard.

　＊　単語の順序も表しているので注意。

・品詞の修飾関係

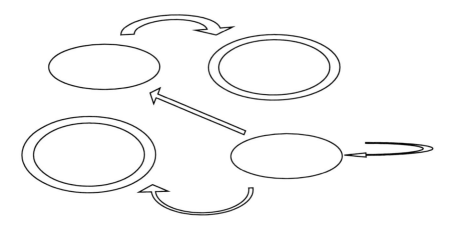

・品詞の修飾関係

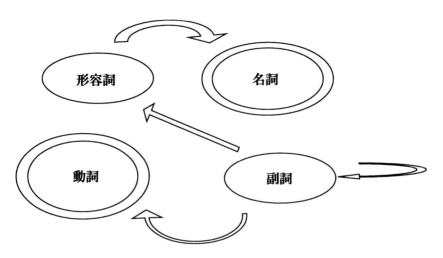

・修飾語とは？
1. 意味的には
   形容詞：物事の状態や性質を表す語
   副詞：①時、②場所、③程度、を表す語
2. 形態的には
   前置詞　＋　a, the, my, your … ＋ 名詞
   （→　形容詞句、副詞句）

・英文の骨組は？／ It の指すものは？

　Kabuki started (**in** 〜に the early 17th century) (**as** 〜として a sort of variety show){performed(**by** 〜によって troupes of itinerant entertainers.)}　(**By** 〜によって the Genroku period,)　it had attained its first flourishing (**as** 〜として a mature theater,)　and it continued, (**through** 〜を通して much of the Edo era,)　to be the most popular form of stage entertainment.　*Kabuki* reached its artistic peak (**with** 〜と共に the magnificient plays of Tsuruya Namboku IV and Kawatake Mokuami.)

・英文の骨組は？／It の指すものは？
　　　→　前置詞（前置詞句）である。
・*Kabuki* started.
　　歌舞伎は始まった。
・It had attained its first flourishing, and it continued to be the most popular form of stage entertainment.
　　歌舞伎は（＝それは）（それの）最初の繁栄期に達していた、そして歌舞伎は（＝それは）最も人気のある舞台芸能の一形態であり続けた。

・*Kabuki* reached **its** artistic peak.
　歌舞伎は<u>その</u>（＝歌舞伎の）芸術的頂点に達した。
　<u>It</u> / <u>its</u> ＝ Kabuki

・構文と意味のチェック　―学生解答＆模範解答―
・*Kabuki* started (**in** the early 17th century)(**as** a sort of variety show){<u>performed</u> (**by** troupes of itinerant entertainers.)}
　歌舞伎は17世紀初期に<u>演じられた</u>さまざまな劇として始まった。
　→　歌舞伎は、（旅芸人の一座によって<u>演じられる</u>）
　（一種の寄席演劇として、）（17世紀初頭に）始まった。

・(**By** the Genroku era,) it <u>had attained</u> **its** first flourishing (**as** a mature theater,)
　元禄時代までには、歌舞伎は発達した劇場として最初に花開くことになり、
　→　（元禄時代までには、）　歌舞伎は（＝それは）（円熟した劇として）（その）最初の繁栄期に<u>達していた</u>。

・and **it** continued, (**through** much of the Edo era,) <u>to be</u> the most popular form of stage entertainment.
　それは続き、江戸時代のほとんどを通じて、最も人気の舞台の娯楽という。
　→　そして歌舞伎は（＝それは）、（江戸時代のほとんどの間、）最も人気のある舞台芸能の一形態で<u>あり</u>続けた。

・*Kabuki* reached **its** artistic peak (**with** the magnificient plays of Tsuruya Nomboku IV and Kawatake Mokuami.)

歌舞伎は四世鶴屋南北と河竹黙阿弥というすばらしい演劇をする人を**伴った**芸術的なものになった。
→　歌舞伎は、(四世鶴屋南北と河竹黙阿弥の見事な演劇／脚本**によって、**)その芸術的頂点に達した。

課題：次の英文の下線部を和訳しなさい。下線部を和訳する際、「上手」、「下手」という語を必ず使用すること。

　The *Kabuki* stage uses a draw curtain.　<u>It has broad, black, green, and orange vertical stripes and is normally drawn open from stage right to stage left accompanied by the striking of wooden clappers.</u>

　<u>Stage left is regarded as the place of honor and is occupied by characters of high rank, guests, and important messengers or official representatives.</u>　Stage right is occupied of low rank and members of a household.

第2章

日本事象・日本地理・日本史の理解

　「第2章　日本事象・日本地理・日本史の理解」では、問題形式で日本事情、日本地理、日本史の知識を英語でどのように表現するのか、学習しましょう。

　問題1　選択肢から適語を選び、次の英文と日本語を結びつけ、番号で答えなさい。≪日本文化事象≫

日本事象-01-1.　____

　They were originally the servants of government officials who were dispatched from the capital to rural communities during the Heian period.　They later became warriors specializing in the martial arts, and eventually some went on to become influential in politics.

日本事象-01-2.　____

　It literally means "The Way of the Bushi" and refers to the Japanese warrior's code of chivalry in the feudal ages.　This code embodied the spirit and principles of morality to which the samurai warriors were supposed to adhere.　It emphasized loyalty, courage, and honor.　The term 'samurai' means 'to serve.'

日本事象-01-3.　____

　It is the early summer rainy season which begins about the middle of July and lasts about a month.　This rain is needed by the farmers at rice-planting time.

日本事象-01-4. ＿＿＿

It is usually translated as generalissimo. It was originally a temporary title given by the emperor to the commander-in-chief of an expeditionary army. Later, it developed into the official title given by the emperor to the administrative head of the country. This shogunate system lasted until the mid-19th century.

日本事象-01-5. ＿＿＿

They are violent tropical storms which often strike Japan from early summer through autumn.

| 1. 梅雨 | 2. 武士道 | 3. 侍 | 4. 台風 | 5. 将軍 |

日本事象-02-1. ＿＿＿

It is a traditional Japanese inn with the interior designed in the traditional Japanese style. The rates usually include breakfast and supper.

日本事象-02-2. ＿＿＿

It is a private home that offers overnight accommodations. It is basically a small inn, and as such it is certified by the public health office.

日本事象-02-3. ＿＿＿

The person is a kimono-clad female entertainer who is trained in the traditional arts, singing, dancing, and conversation and who serves as a party companion and hostess.

日本事象-02-4. ____
It is Japan's highest mountain with a height of 3,776 meters. Though classified as an active volcano, it last erupted about 300 years ago. Its almost perfect cone shape is world-famous for its beauty and the mountain is a symbol of Japan.

日本事象-02-5. ____
It is the super-express train nicknamed "The Bullet Train." It first began operating in 1964, the year of the Tokyo Olympics, and now has lines extending from Tokyo to the southern island of Kyushu and northern Honshu.

| 1. 新幹線 | 2. 富士山 | 3. 芸者 | 4. 民宿 | 5. 旅館 |

日本事象-03-1. ____
It is a fermented alcoholic beverage made from rice. It has a distinctive aroma and can be served hot or cold. The alcohol content ranges from 15 to 20 percent.

日本事象-03-02. ____
It literally means "circulating sushi." Plates of sushi are set on a conveyor belt encircling the serving bar, and as the plates pass by, the customers select what they want. Prices for kaiten-zushi are generally lower than at regular sushi restaurants.

日本事象-03-3. ____

It is a dish of thinly sliced beef, onions, tofu, and shiitake mushrooms cooked in a pan at the table. Sugar, soy sauce, and sake are added for flavor.

日本事象-03-4. ____

They are seafood and vegetables that are dipped in batter, deep-fried and served with a special sauce.

日本事象-03-5. ____

It is a Japanese-style tavern that serves a wide range of food and drinks at relatively low prices. It is popular with mostly office workers and young people.

1. 回転寿司	2. 酒	3. 居酒屋	4. すきやき	5. 天ぷら

日本事象-04-1. ____

It is a traditional stage drama performed exclusively by men to the accompaniment of songs and music. It is characterized by a combination of rhythmical words, dancing, elaborate costumes, and stage sets.

日本事象-04-2. ____

It is a genre of the ancient ceremonial dances and music of the Imperial Court. The term bugaku refers to the dances, while kangen refers to the music performed by an ensemble of wind, string, and percussion instruments.

日本事象-04-3. ____

It is a classical stage art performed exclusively by men to the accompaniment of recitative chants called yokyoku and an orchestra consisting of a flute and three types of drums. It is characterized by symbolic, highly stylized acting, and elaborate masks.

日本事象-04-4. ____

It is a classical puppet play performed to the accompaniment of musical ballads known as joruri. Its charm lies in the harmony of skilled puppeteers and the voices of the joruri singer.

日本事象-04-5. ____

It is a type of music characterized by sentimental ballads of love, broken hearts, parting, and home. Like country music in the U.S., it has a distinctive melodic and singing style. It is especially popular among older age groups.

| 1. 歌舞伎 | 2. 能 | 3. 雅楽 | 4. 演歌 | 5. 文楽 |

日本事象-05-1. ____

It is the Japanese art of calligraphy. Particular emphasis is placed on the shades of the ink, the movement of the writing brush, and the combination of the strokes. It is practiced to cultivate one's inner self.

日本事象-05-2. ____

It is the traditional Japanese art of arranging flowers. In its earlier stages of development, it was closely related to the tea ceremony, being used as a special technique for decorating the tearoom.

日本事象-05-3. ____

It is the art and ritual of serving special powdered tea. It originated in the monasteries of Zen Buddhism, but today it is regarded as a form of artistic discipline for the cultivation of mental composure and elegant manners.

日本事象-05-4. ____

It is a very compact but evocative verse form of 17 syllables in a 5-7-5 line pattern. Its themes may be inspired by intuitive perception into nature and life.

日本事象-05-5. ____

It is a style of wood-block printing developed during the Edo period. It depicts the Japanese landscape, the everyday life of commoners, kabuki actors, sumo wrestlers, and beautiful women.

| 1. 茶の湯 | 2. 浮世絵 | 3. 俳句 | 4. 書道 | 5. 生け花 |

日本事象-06-1. ____

It was developed as a form of unarmed self-defense, but is now a popular sport. Its main concept is the skillful use of balance and timing to turn an opponent's strength against him or her.

日本事象-06-2. ____

It is a form of unarmed self-defense which originated in Okinawa. It is characterized by sharp, quick blows delivered with the hands and feet.

日本事象-06-3. ____

It is a time-honored Japanese style of wrestling. Two contestants are matched against one another in a ring. One contestant loses when any part of his body other than the soles of his feet touches the ground or when he is pushed out of the ring.

日本事象-06-4. ____

It is the act of singing through an amplifier to recorded musical accompaniment. Most bars and pubs have very sophisticated systems of it.

日本事象-06-5. ____

It is a game of chance and skill played on an upright pinball machine. A player tries to manipulate small steel balls through certain holes so as to win more balls which can later be exchanged for such prizes as cigarettes, candy, or other items.

| 1. 柔道 | 2. 相撲 | 3. カラオケ | 4. 空手 | 5. パチンコ |

日本事象-07-1. ____

It is a Shinto shrine where a particular kami (Shinto deity) is enshrined. People visit it to make wedding vows, celebrate births and the New Year, and make prayers. Most festivals in Japan are held in dedication to the kami of the local shrine.

日本事象-07-2. ____

It is a Buddhist temple where funerals, memorial services, and other events are conducted. Many of them are popular tourist attractions for their Buddhist statues, artifacts, and buildings of historical importance.

日本事象-07-3. ____

It is Confucianism, formulated by Confucius, a philosopher in ancient China. It teaches ethics with an emphasis on ancestor worship and devotion to parents, family and friends. Combined with it and Buddhism, it has exerted great influence on the spiritual and cultural life of the Japanese.

日本事象-07-4. ____

It is the indigenous religion of Japan. It is polytheistic, and its gods are worshiped at shrines called jinja. It has neither a specific founder nor any books of scripture.

日本事象-07-5. ____

It is Buddhism, founded in India and introduced through China and Korea to Japan in the 6th century. It teaches a way to enlighten and has exerted great influence on the spiritual and cultural life of the Japanese.

| 1. 儒教　　2. 寺　　3. 神社　　4. 仏教　　5. 神道 |

日本事象-08-1. ____

It is the celebration of the New Year and is the most important holiday in Japan, comparable to Christmas in Western countries. Entrances of houses and buildings are decorated with a set of pine branches and bamboos. A sweet sake called toso, and a soup called zoni are served during the holiday.

日本事象-08-2. ____

It is a festival to celebrate the growth of children. On November 15, girls of seven, boys of five and three-year-old children of either sex are taken to shrines by their parents to give thanks and pray for divine blessing.

日本事象-08-3. ____

They are the weeks centering around the vernal equinox and autumnal equinox. During these periods, Buddhist temples hold special services and people pay their respects at their ancestors' graves.

日本事象-08-4. ____

It is "cherry blossom viewing." In spring, when the cherry blossoms are in full bloom, people picnic under the trees. Sometimes the parties last late into the night and can become quite lively.

日本事象-08-5. ____

It is a three-day Buddhist holiday, usually August 13, 14, and 15. During this time the spirits of the dead are said to return to their former homes and families. People light lanterns to guide the spirits and perform bon dances for their entertainment. The week of it is considered bon-yasumi, or bon vacation, and many people return to their hometowns or take trips.

| 1. 正月 | 2. 花見 | 3. お盆 | 4. 七五三 | 5. 彼岸 |

日本事象-09-1. ____

It is a neighborhood bathhouse open to the public for a fee. It is divided into two parts according to sex, and each part is equipped with a dressing room and a large bathtub along with one or two smaller ones. Though decreasing in number, it is still popular as a gathering place, particularly among senior citizens.

日本事象-09-2. ____

It is a light cotton kimono for summer wear. It is used for general relaxation and as sleeping wear. It is also commonly worn at some summer events such as local festivals and fireworks displays.

日本事象-09-3. ____

It is the long robe with wide sleeves and a broad sash that is traditionally worn as an outer garment by Japanese.

日本事象-09-4. ____

It is the ceremonial exchange of betrothal gifts between the families of an engaged couple. The gifts include money and such things as seaweed, dried squid, and bonito which are symbolic of happiness.

日本事象-09-5. ____

It is an arranged meeting with a prospective marriage partner and is a common practice in Japan. It is first arranged by a go-between, usually a mature man or woman of good social standing, but subsequent dates, if any, are agreed on by the couple themselves. A couple may date several times before deciding whether or not to take the step into marriage.

| 1. 浴衣 | 2. 着物 | 3. お見合い | 4. 結納 | 5. 銭湯 |

日本事象-10-1. ____

It is a cram school where students take lessons in addition to their regular schoolwork so as to be ready for entrance examinations to junior high schools, high schools, or universities.

日本事象-10-2. ____

They are the Chinese ideographs or characters on which the Japanese writing system is based. Each one is a symbol for a concept and is used for writing content words or root elements. They are used in combination with kana, which are phonetic characters that represent syllables.

日本事象-10-3. ____

The former refers to one's true feelings or motives, whereas the latter is the face one wears in public. The former may be expressed privately, while the latter is an opinion designed for social acceptance.

日本事象-10-4. ____

The former refers to an aesthetic of refined rusticity, and the latter refers to the elegant serenity of desolation. They are among the highest of aesthetic qualities valued in traditional Japanese arts, particularly the tea ceremony and haiku.

日本事象-10-5. ____

It is a school excursion to places of historical interest or scenic beauty. Such a trip is usually made three times, once each in elementary, junior high and high school.

1. わび・さび　　2. 本音・建前　　3. 塾　　4. 修学旅行
5. 漢字

問題2　日本語を参考に、選択肢から番号を選び、次の英文を完成させなさい。≪地理≫

1. 北海道地方：日本列島の一番北にあり、動植物の分布は本州と異なる。広大な山岳、原野が広がり、景色は雄大で温泉や湖が多い。また、日本列島の先住民ともいわれる、アイヌの部落もみられる。

２．東北地方：山・湖・高原・温泉などの景勝地が多い。各地に地方色豊かな行事や民謡・踊りなど有名な郷土芸能が数多く残っている。

３．関東地方：箱根・伊香保など山と湖に囲まれた有名な温泉がある。房総・三浦の両半島には、海の景勝地が多く、また、東照宮のある日光、湿原の尾瀬など特色ある観光地もある。

４．中部地方：富士山を初め、アルプスの山々・高原・渓谷などに恵まれ、多くの保養地・温泉・スキー場などがある。

５．近畿地方：長い間、日本の政治・文化の中心であった奈良や京都があり、琵琶湖・紀伊半島・日本海沿岸など、美しい景色に恵まれたところが多い。

６．中国・四国地方：瀬戸内海には、海と山の景勝地が多い。山陰地方には、日本神話のふるさとの出雲や鳥取の砂丘、それに、有名な温泉が各地にある。

７．九州地方：日本列島の西南端にあたり、明るい空と海、暖かい気候に恵まれている。亜熱帯植物のある青島・大隅半島や阿蘇山・霧島山・雲仙岳などの雄大な火山があり、温泉も多い。

地理-01.
(   ), the northernmost island of the Japanese archipelago, has a flora and fauna that are different from those of Honshu, the main island. The scenery there is truly majestic, with imposing mountains and wide plains, and many hot springs and lakes. There are also settlements of Ainu, who are

said to be the first settlers of the Japanese islands.

| 1. Hokkaido | 2. Tohoku | 3. Kanto | 4. Chubu |
| 5. Kinki | 6. Chugoku and Shikoku | 7. Kyushu |

地理-02.

(　　　　　　　　) has many scenic mountains, lakes, highlands and hot springs. Many localities still annually hold events peculiar to their own area, and a considerable number of the region's fold-singing and dancing styles, some of which have become famous as examples of rural performing arts, have kept alive till this day.

| 1. Hokkaido | 2. Tohoku | 3. Kanto | 4. Chubu |
| 5. Kinki | 6. Chugoku and Shikoku | 7. Kyushu |

地理-03.

(　　　　　　　　) has several famous mountain-and lake-surrounded hot spring resorts, such as Hakone and Ikaho. Many picturesque spots can be found along the coast of the Boso and Miura peninsulas, and the region also has sightseeing places with a special attraction of their own, such as the Tosho Shrine in Nikko, and the Oze marshland.

| 1. Hokkaido | 2. Tohoku | 3. Kanto | 4. Chubu |
| 5. Kinki | 6. Chugoku and Shikoku | 7. Kyushu |

地理-04.

(　　　　　　　　　) is blessed not only with Mt. Fuji, but also with the mountains of the Japan Alps and with highlands and valleys. There are many health resorts, hot springs and ski resorts in this region.

1. Hokkaido　2. Tohoku　3. Kanto　4. Chubu
5. Kinki　6. Chugoku and Shikoku　7. Kyushu

地理-05.

(　　　　　　　　　) has the ancient cities of Nara and Kyoto, which were for long the political and cultural centers of Japan. There are also many places of great scenic beauty, such as Lake Biwa, the Kii Peninsula and the coast of Japan Sea.

1. Hokkaido　2. Tohoku　3. Kanto　4. Chubu
5. Kinki　6. Chugoku and Shikoku　7. Kyushu

地理-06.

(　　　　　　　　　) bound the Seto Inland Sea with its picturesque blend of ocean and mountain scenery. In the San-in region are Izumo, the scene of many of the Japanese myths, and the sand dunes of Tottori. The region is also dotted with famous hot springs.

1. Hokkaido　2. Tohoku　3. Kanto　4. Chubu
5. Kinki　6. Chugoku and Shikoku　7. Kyushu

地理-07.
　(　　　　　　　　), the main southern island of the Japanese archipelago, has bright skies and seas and is blessed with a warm climate. On Ao lsland and the Osumi Peninsula can be found semi-tropical vegetation. There are also many imposing volcanoes, such as Aso, Kirishima and Unzendake. Here, too, hot springs are numerous.

1. Hokkaido	2. Tohoku	3. Kanto	4. Chubu
5. Kinki	6. Chugoku and Shikoku		7. Kyushu

問題3　日本語を参考に、選択肢から番号を選び、次の英文を完成させなさい。≪歴史文化≫

歴史文化-01.
　奈良は、8世紀に約70年間続いた古都である。神社、仏閣、仏像、絵画など国宝や重要文化財の宝庫である。

　The ancient city of (　　　　　　　) was the capital of Japan for about seventy years, starting the early eighth century. With its many shrines, Buddhist temples, statues of Buddha, carvings and paintings, it is rich in National Treasures and Important Cultural Assets.

1. Nara	2. Todai Temple	3. Horyu Temple
4. Kyoto	5. Kamakura	6. Himeji Castle

歴史文化-02.

　高さ 16.91m（53.18 フィート）の有名な奈良の大仏（752 年開眼、その後度々修復）がある東大寺や、五重塔が猿沢池に美しい影をうつす興福寺、さらに放し飼いの鹿が沢山いる春日神社などが、とくに有名である。また、東大寺に正倉院という特殊な防湿構造（校倉「あぜくら」造りという）の木造倉庫がある。ここには、当時の天皇の遺愛品、東大寺の寺宝・文書など奈良時代の美術品のほか、中国やペルシアなどからの伝来品 9,000 余点が収められている。

　奈良国立博物館は、仏教美術の粋を集めている点で日本第一である。

　Particularly famous are Nara's (　　　　　　) with its 16.21-meter-high (53.18feet) statue of Buddha (dedicated in the year 752 and renovated several times since), Kofuku Temple with its five-storied pagoda facing the beautiful pond called Sarusawa-no-ike, and Kasuga Shrine with its many tame deer which are allowed to roam free. Todai Temple also has the Shoso-in, a wooden treasure-house with a special construction (called azekura) which is resistant to moisture. Stored in this are more than nine thousand items, including fine art objects which belonged to the emperor of that time, Todai Temple treasures and manuscripts of the Nara period, plus items which came from countries such as China and Persia.

　As far as assembling the cream of Buddhist art goes, Nara National Museum is without a peer in Japan.

1. Nara	2. Todai Temple	3. Horyu Temple
4. Kyoto	5. Kamakura	6. Himeji Castle

歴史文化-03.

奈良近郊には、現存する世界最古の木造建築である法隆寺がある。また、隣接する飛鳥地方は、6～7世紀頃、日本文化の開花した地方で、日本仏教の発祥地でもあり、天皇の御陵や古墳・史跡などが点在している。

1972年に、極彩色の壁画が発見されて有名になった高松塚古墳もこの一角にある。

On the outskirts of Nara is (　　　　　), the world's oldest wooden structures still in existence. Also, the nearby Asuka district was where the culture of Japan flowered around the sixth and seventh centuries, and as such was the cradle of Japanese Buddhism; in this area can be found Imperial tombs, burial mounds and historical relics.

One such place is Takamatsuzuka, which became famous when a tumulus with brilliantly colored wall paintings was discovered in 1972.

1. Nara	2. Todai Temple	3. Horyu Temple
4. Kyoto	5. Kamakura	6. Himeji Castle

歴史文化-04.

京都は、8世紀末から約1000年余り皇居のあった古都である。

また、東山、嵐山、嵯峨野、加茂川など景勝地も多く、西陣織、友禅染、京人形、清水焼、京扇子などの名産品もある。

The ancient city of (　　　　　) was the Imperial seat for more than a thousand years, starting at the end of the eighth century.

In addition, there are many places of scenic beauty, such as Mt. Higashiyama, Arashiyama, Sagano and the River Kamo, and many famous local products, such as Nishijin brocade, yuzen dyed fabrics, Kyo dolls, Kiyomizu ware and Kyo fans.

1. Nara	2. Todai Temple	3. Horyu Temple
4. Kyoto	5. Kamakura	6. Himeji Castle

歴史文化-05.
　東京近郊の鎌倉は、12世紀末から約150年間、武家政権の所在地となったところである。鶴岡八幡宮、長谷の大仏、建長寺、円覚寺などの史跡が多い。

　(　　　　　　　　), which is not far from Tokyo, became the seat of the military government for a period of one hundred and fifty years, starting from the end of the twelfth century. The many historical places that can be seen there include Tsurugaoka Hachiman Shrine, the Great Buddha of Hase, Kencho Temple and Engaku Temple.

1. Nara	2. Todai Temple	3. Horyu Temple
4. Kyoto	5. Kamakura	6. Himeji Castle

歴史文化-06.
　姫路城は、14世紀中頃につくられ、その後次第に拡張され、その規模の雄大さ、純白の天守閣の美しさなどで、一頭地を抜いている。別名、白鷺城とも呼ばれる。

(　　　　　　　　) was built in the middle of the fourteenth century and was gradually enlarged until now. It is unrivaled for its size as well as for the beauty of its pure white tower. Another name it is known by is Shirasagi Castle.

1. Nara	2. Todai Temple	3. Horyu Temple
4. Kyoto	5. Kamakura	6. Himeji Castle

歴史文化-07.

　城郭の石垣の積み石は、重さ1トン前後のものが多いが、大阪城にはとくに大きなものが使用されている。大阪城の石は、遠く110 km（68マイル）もはなれた小豆島から運ばれたもので、とくに重い石の場合は、海中に石をつるし、浮力分だけ軽くして運ぶ石釣船が使われたという。

Most of the stones of the terraced walls of castles weigh about 1 ton each, but the stones of (　　　　　　　　) are particularly large. These stones had to be brought 110 kilometers (68 miles) from Shodo Island, and it is said that particularly large stones were suspended in the sea so that the buoyancy lightened them slightly, making it easier for the boats to transport them.

1. Osaka Castle　　2. Edo Castle
3. non-collectable loans　　4. coalition party
5. privatizing public highway corporations and the postal service
6. the Democratic Party

歴史文化-08.

皇居は、徳川時代の将軍の居城であった江戸城の跡で、毎年1月2日と天皇誕生日には、国民参賀が行われるので、その一部が参観できる。

The present Imperial Palace was built on the site of (　　　　　　　　　　), headquarters of the feudal government in the Tokugawa era. A part of it can be visited on the second day of each year and on the Emperor's birthday, at which times people are allowed to enter in order to offer their congratulations to the Emperor.

---

1. Osaka Castle　　2. Edo Castle
3. non-collectable loans　　4. coalition party
5. privatizing public highway corporations and the postal service
6. the Democratic Party

歴史文化-09.

昭和の終わりに発生したバブル経済は、1991年に入る一気にしぼみはじめます。地価は下がり、株価も急速に下がり、特に、バブル時代に不動産向けの融資を拡大し続けた銀行は、膨大な**不良債権**を抱え込むことになりました。経営破綻した銀行も出て、預金者に大きな不安を与えることになりましたので、政府は60兆円もの資金を導入して、金融システムを保護する策をとりました。しかし、製造業は不景気の風をまともに受けてリストラを余儀なくされ、倒産も相継ぎ、失業者が世に溢れだしました。アメリカ、イギリスでは年々失業率が減っていくのに対して、日本では次第に上昇して、2003年10月には失業率

が 5.2%前後にまで上がりました。

The "bubble economy" that formed at the end of the Showa period suddenly collapsed in 1991. Land prices fell, stock prices collapsed and, most notably, banks that had extended financing for real estate during the bubble found themselves with huge amounts of (   ). After a few banks went bankrupt, resulting in a great deal of uncertainty among depositors, the government stepped in to protect the banking system with 60 trillion yen. But the manufacturing sector took the depression head on and was forced to restructure to survive. A string of bankruptcies occurred creating large-scale unemployment. While the unemployment rate for the United States and the United Kingdom shrunk year by year, the Japan's unemployed increased, and in October 2003 the rate reached around 5.2%.

---

1. Osaka Castle　　2. Edo Castle
3. non-collectable loans　　4. coalition party
5. privatizing public highway corporations and the postal service
6. the Democratic Party

歴史文化-10.
　自民党の政治の**腐敗**、政治改革への取り組みの**怠慢**に対する一般市民の憤りで、1993年には、日本新党の細川護煕を首相にした**連立政権**が誕生したものの、1996年には自民党が勢力を盛り返し、再び権力の座につきました。その自民党の勢力下、2000年になっても景気が回復する気配はありませんでした。

Due to the anger of the general population with corruption in Liberal Democratic Party and a negligent attitude toward government reform, a new (　　　　　　　　) under Japan New Party of Morihiro Hosokawa took over, but Liberal Democratic Party recovered and returned to power in 1996. Again under Liberal Democratic Party, the economy showed little sign of recovery still in 2000.

1. Osaka Castle　　2. Edo Castle
3. non-collectable loans　　4. coalition party
5. privatizing public highway corporations and the postal service
6. the Democratic Party

歴史文化-11.
　2001年、自民党の古い体質からの脱却、**構造改革**、景気の回復、**道路公団**や**郵政事業**の民営化などをうたって、自民党、保守新党、公明党との連立のもと、小泉純一郎が首相となりました。

In 2001, with promises that included changing the old ways of Liberal Democratic Party, implementing structural reform, improving the economy, and (　　　　　　　　), a coalition party was formed between LDP, New Conservative Party and Komeito with Junichiro Koizumi as the prime minister.

1. Osaka Castle　　2. Edo Castle
3. non-collectable loans　　4. coalition party
5. privatizing public highway corporations and the postal service
6. the Democratic Party

歴史文化-12.
しかし、依然として日本経済は上向きにならず、道路公団の民営化も中途半端。世論では2大政党による政権の交代、指示の活性化を求める声が高まり、2003年11月の総選挙では、選挙の前に自民党と合体した民主党が大幅に議席を増やしました。しかし、社民党や共産党が議席を減らしましたので、野党が連立を組んで政権を奪うまでにはいたらず、引き続き小泉純一郎が首相の座にとどまることになりました。

2006年9月、安倍晋三が新たな首相となったが、国の財政赤字の解消、**年金制度**の立て直しなどなど、21世紀の課題は山積みです。

However, Japan's economy failed to improve, and the move to privatize public highway corporations stumbled. The calls for a more active government increased, and a November 2003 general election resulted in a significant increase in the number of Diet seats held by (　　　　　　　　　　) united with Liberal Party. However, Social Democratic Party and Japanese Communist Party both lost seats, and so the opposition coalition was unable to secure enough seats to take power, allowing Junichiro Koizumi to remain prime minister.

In 2006, Shinzo Abe became the new prime minister, but he faces such lingering challenges as reducing the national debt and rebuilding the pension system.

---

1. Osaka Castle　　2. Edo Castle
3. non-collectable loans　　4. coalition party
5. privatizing public highway corporations and the postal service
6. the Democratic Party

第3章

英文解釈 ―多読・速読―

「第3章 英文解釈 ―多読・速読―」では、多読・速読に必要な内容を学習しましょう。「考えるべき事柄」と「その解答」をセットで述べる形式で進んでいます。

問題：次の英文を読み、下記の設問に答えなさい。

(1) <u>One area of confusion when talking about immigrants is deciding who exactly is a foreigner.</u> Here the key distinction is between someone who is 'foreign-born' and someone who has a foreign nationality — that is, who travels on a passport issued by another country. Any immigrant who naturalizes as a citizen of their new country ceases to be a 'foreigner' at once, but he or she will always be foreign-born.

According to the US census for 1990, 7.9% of the population were foreign-born, but only 4.7% were still foreigners because the rest had become naturalized citizens. This means that the proportion of foreigners will depend in some degree on (2) [become, how, to, is, a, it, citizen, easy]. In France, for example, the proportion of residents who are foreigners has remained rather stable since 1975, at 6 to 7%, but the proportion who are foreign-born is probably about 11%. In Germany on the other hand, naturalization has traditionally been more difficult so the proportion of foreigners remains (　(3)　).

A further complication is that some people look on anyone belonging to an ethnic minority as an immigrant, even if they have been born in that country. In the United Kingdom around 6% of the population belong to a minority ethnic group. The foreign-born however are only 4%, and many of those are 'white' people who have come from Europe, Australia and elsewhere.

問1. 下線部(1)を日本語に直しなさい。

問2. (2)の[　　]内の語を、意味の通るように並べ換えなさい。
_____

問3. 空欄(3)に入るべき最も適切な語は、次の(ア)〜(エ)のどれか、記号を○で囲みなさい。
　(ア) lower　　(イ) higher　　(ウ) stable　　(エ) unstable

問4. 本文によると、一般に「外国人」と呼ばれる人々が3種類いる。その3種類の人たちを簡潔に述べなさい。
　①_____　②_____　③_____

・スキミング（飛ばし読み―大意をつかむ―）の仕方は？

・スキャニング（情報検索読み―必要な情報を読み取る―）の仕方は？

・スキミング（飛ばし読み―大意をつかむ―）の仕方は？
5 W 1 H: Who(- Whom), When, Where, What, Why, How

・スキャニング(情報検索読み－必要な情報を読み取る－)の仕方は？
5 W 1 H: Who(- Whom), When, Where, What, Why, How の中で問題で問われているものを探す。

・スキャニング(情報検索読み－必要な情報を読み取る)の仕方は？
5 W 1 H: Who(- Whom), When, Where, What, Why, How の中で問題で問われているものを探す。

1. Foreigner
2. ３種類の「外国人」がいる
3. 帰化した者、外国出生者、合衆国、フランス、英国

(1) One area of confusion when talking about <u>immigrants</u> is
              (Who)
<u>deciding who exactly is a foreigner.</u> Here the key distinction is
   (What)   (Who)
between someone who is '<u>foreign-born</u>' and someone who has a
          (How)
<u>foreign nationality</u> — that is, who <u>travels on a passport issued by</u>
  (How)   (How)
<u>another country.</u> <u>Any immigrant who naturalizes as a citizen</u>

<u>of their new country ceases to be a 'foreigner' at once, but he or she</u>
            (Why)
<u>will always be foreign-born.</u>

According to the US census for 1990, 7.9% of the population were
 (Where)
foreign-born, but only 4.7 % were still foreigners because the rest

had become naturalized citizens.　This means that the proportion

of foreigners will depend in some degree on [become, how, to, is, a,

it, citizen, easy].　In France, for example, the proportion of
 (Where)
residents who are foreigners has remained rather stable since

1975, at 6 to 7%, but the proportion who are foreign-born is

probably about 11%.　In Germany on the other hand,
 (Where)
naturalization has traditionally been more difficult so the

proportion of foreigners remains (　(3)　).

　A further complication is that some people look on anyone

belonging to an ethnic minority as an immigrant, even if they have
 (Who)　　　　　　　　(Who)
been born in that country.　In the United Kingdom around 6% of
 (Who)　　　　　　　　　　(Where)
the population belong to a minority ethnic group.　The foreign-born
 (Who)

41

however are only 4%, and many of those are 'white' people who

have come from Europe, Australia and elsewhere.

Who: foreigner, immigrant = ethnic minority / minority ethnic
 group (← even if they have been born in that country)
What: deciding who exactly is a foreigner
How: foreign-born, foreign nationality
 (→ travels on a passport issued by another country)
Why: Any immigrant who naturalizes as a citizen of their new country immediately ceases to be a 'foreigner' but he or she will always be foreign-born.
Where: the US (7.9% = foreign-born, 4.7 % = foreigners, the rest = naturalized citizens)
 France (foreigners = 6 to 7%, foreign-born = 11%)
 Germany (naturalization — more difficult, foreigners — ((3))
 the United Kingdom (6% = minority ethnic group, foreign-born = 4%)
 (← many of those are 'white' people who have come from Europe, Australia and elsewhere.)

・Foreigner とは?

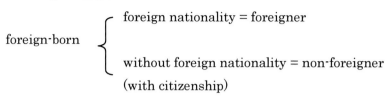

問4. 本文によると、一般に「外国人」と呼ばれる人々が3種類いる。その3種類の人たちを簡潔に述べなさい。

① <u>外国出生者（＝外国生まれの人）</u>　② <u>外国籍の人</u>
③ <u>少数民族の移民（たとえその国で生まれて、その国の国籍を取得していても）</u>

・Foreigner とは?

country＼nationality	foreign-born	foreign nationality (→ foreigner)	naturalization (→ naturalized citizen)
the US	7.9%	4.7%	?
France	11%	6〜7%	?
Germany	—	lower / higher / stable / unstable	more difficult
the United Kingdom	4%	—	—

・Foreigner とは?

nationality \ country	foreign-born	foreign nationality (→foreigner)	naturalization (→ naturalized citizen)
the US	7.9%	4.7%	**3.2%**
France	11%	6〜7%	**4〜5%**
Germany	—	lower / higher / stable / unstable	more difficult
the United Kingdom	4%	—	—

※ foreign-born = foreign nationality + naturalization
　　　　　　　　　(→ foreigner)　　　(→ naturalized citizen)

問 3. 空欄(3)に入るべき最も適切な語は、次の（ア）〜（エ）のどれか、記号を○で囲みなさい。
（ア）lower　(イ) higher　（ウ）stable　（エ）unstable

・紛らわしい文法事項

One area of confusion when talking about immigrants is deciding who exactly is a foreigner. Here the key distinction is between someone who is 'foreign-born' and someone who has a foreign nationality — that is, who travels on a passport issued by another country. Any immigrant who naturalizes as a citizen of their new country ceases to be a 'foreigner' at once, but he or she will always be foreign-born.

According to the US census for 1990, 7.9% of the population were foreign-born, but only 4.7 % were still foreigners because the rest had become naturalized citizens. This means that the proportion of foreigners will depend in some degree on [become, how, to, is, a, it, citizen, easy]. In France, for example, the proportion of residents who are foreigners has remained rather stable since 1975, at 6 to 7%, but the proportion who are foreign-born is probably about 11%. In Germany on the other hand, naturalization has traditionally been more difficult so the proportion of foreigners remains higher.

A further complication is that some people look on anyone belonging to an ethnic minority as an immigrant, even if they have been born in that country. In the United Kingdom around 6% of the population belong to a minority ethnic group. The foreign-born however are only 4%, and many of those are 'white' people who have come from Europe, Australia and elsewhere.

1. 過去形（-ed：～した）なのか
   過去分詞（-ed：～されて）なのか

2. 現在分詞（-ing：～してして／～する）なのか
   動名詞（-ing：～すること）なのか

3. It の示すものは何か
   ①もの（具体的には何か）なのか
   ②不定詞（ to 動詞： ～すること）なのか

4. and の働きは何か
   何と何を結びつけているのか
   ①文（S+V…）と文（S+V…）を結びつけているのか

②単語と単語を結びつけているのか（a, b, c, ...and z）

5. **that** は何か
   ①指示語（それ、その、…）なのか
   ②接続詞（〜ということ）なのか
   ③関係代名詞、関係副詞（訳はない）なのか

・**紛らわしい文法事項**

One area of confusion when talking about immigrants is deciding who exactly is a foreigner. Here the key distinction is between someone who is 'foreign-born' and someone who has a foreign nationality — that is, who travels on a passport issued by another country. Any immigrant who naturalizes as a citizen of their new country ceases to be a 'foreigner' at once, but he or she will always be foreign-born.

According to the US census for 1990, 7.9% of the population were foreign-born, but only 4.7 % were still foreigners because the rest had become naturalized citizens. This means that the proportion of foreigners will depend in some degree on [become, how, to, is, a, it, citizen, easy]. In France, for example, the proportion of residents who are foreigners has remained rather stable since 1975, at 6 to 7%, but the proportion who are foreign-born is probably about 11%. In Germany on the other hand, naturalization has traditionally been more difficult so the proportion of foreigners remains higher.

A further complication is that some people look on anyone belonging to an ethnic minority as an immigrant, even if they have been born in that country. In the United Kingdom around 6% of the population belong to a minority ethnic group. The <u>foreign-born</u> however are only 4%, and many of those are 'white' people <u>who have come</u> from Europe, Australia and elsewhere.

1. 過去形（-ed：〜した）なのか
   過去分詞（-ed：〜されて）なのか　　　　issued, foreign-born,
   　　　　　　　　　　　　　　　　　　　　　　　naturalized, born
   　　　　　　　　　　　　had become（過去完了形）
   　　　　　　　　　　　has remained（現在完了形）
   　　　　　　　　has been / **have** been（現在完了形）
   　　　　　　　　　　　　have come（現在完了形）

2. 現在分詞（-ing：〜してして／〜する）なのか　　talking
   動名詞（-ing：〜すること）なのか　　　　　　　deciding

3. It の示すものは何か？
   ①もの（具体的には何か）なのか
   ②不定詞（**to** 動詞：〜すること）なのか　　**it** = to become

4. **and** の働きは何か
   何と何を結びつけているのか
   ①文（S+V…）と文（S+V…）を結びつけているのか
   　　　　　　　　　　The foreign-born … 4% **and**
   　　　　　　　　　　many of those are 'white' …
   ②単語と単語を結びつけているのか（a, b, c, …**and** z）
   　　　　　　　　　　someone who is 'foreign-born' **and**
   　　　　　　　　　　someone who has a foreign …

Europe, Australia, **and** elsewhere.

5. **that** は何か
   ①指示語（それ、その...）なのか　　　that is：つまり（熟語）
   ②接続詞（〜ということ）なのか
   　　　　　　　　　　　This means **that** the proportion …
   　　　　　　　　　　　A further complication is **that** …
   ③関係代名詞、関係副詞（訳はない）なのか
   ※ 疑問代名詞（who：誰が）と関係代名詞の主格（who：訳はない）にも注意してください。
   疑問代名詞：
   ・**who** exactly is a foreigner
   関係代名詞（主格）：
   ・someone **who** is 'foreign-born'
   ・someone **who** has a foreign nationality
   ・**who** travels on a passport（先行詞は someone）
   ・Any immigrant **who** nationalizes
   ・residents **who** are foreigners
   ・the proportion （of residents 省略）**who** are foreign-born
   ・'white' people **who** have come

問2. (2)の[　　]内の語を、意味の通るように並べ換えなさい。
<u>how easy it is to become a citizen</u>

どれほど簡単だろうか、市民になることは
→　いかに簡単か、市民になることは
→　市民になることはいかに簡単か

間接疑問文：*疑問詞＋副詞＋主語＋動詞 ～.*
訳：疑問詞、副詞に、主語は動詞にするか。

課題：次の英文をすべて訳しなさい。

① One area of confusion when talking about immigrants is deciding who exactly is a foreigner.

② Here the key distinction is between someone who is 'foreign-born' and someone who has a foreign nationality — that is, who travels on a passport issued by another country.

③ Any immigrant who naturalizes as a citizen of their new country ceases to be a 'foreigner' at once, but he or she will always be foreign-born.

④ According to the US census for 1990, 7.9% of the population were foreign-born, but only 4.7 % were still foreigners because the rest had become naturalized citizens.

⑤ This means that the proportion of foreigners will depend in some degree on **how easy it is to become a citizen.**

⑥ In France, for example, the proportion of residents who are foreigners has remained fairly stable since 1975, at 6 to 7%, but the proportion who are foreign-born is probably around 11%.

⑦ In Germany on the other hand, naturalization has traditionally been more difficult so the proportion of foreigners remains **higher**.

⑧ A further complication is that some people regard anyone belonging to an ethnic minority as an immigrant, even if they have been born in that country.

⑨ In the United Kingdom around 6% of the population belong to a minority ethnic group.

⑩ The foreign-born however are only 4%, and many of those are 'white' people who have come from Europe, Australia and elsewhere.

第4章

日本史（応用）の理解

「第4章　日本史（応用）の理解」では、第2章の日本史の理解からさらに深い内容で、日本史の知識を英語でどのように表現するのか、学習しましょう。

問題　日本語を参考に、選択肢から番号を選び、次の英文を完成させなさい。≪歴史応用≫

奈良・平安-01-1.
　奈良時代は8世紀の大部分、710年から794年の間、現在の奈良に都が置かれていた時代です。この都を平城京と呼びます。
　奈良時代には**中央集権**となり、律令制度が敷かれます。

　The Nara period spans most of the eighth century, from 710 to 794, marking the years when the present-day city of Nara was the seat of the capital. This capital was called (　　　　　).
　The Nara period saw the centralization of power and the implementation of the ritsuryo (legal codes) system of government.

1. Heijokyo
2. Buddhhism
3. Heian
4. Taira
5. Genji

奈良・平安-01-2.

　6世紀半ばには日本に伝わった**仏教**はこの時代に政府に保護されて、大いに栄えました。現存する銅製の**仏像**では世界最大の、東大寺の大仏が作られたのもこの時代です。

　また、中国の唐に何度も人を派遣するなど海外との交流も盛んな時代で、唐の文化を中心に、朝鮮の文化やインド、ペルシアの文化の影響も見られる時代です。

(　　　　　　　　　) flourished in the middle of the sixth century in Japan under the protection of the state. It was during this period that the world's largest existing bronze sculpture of Buddha — the Great Buddha of Todaiji temple — was built.

Foreign interaction thrived during this period, with a number of embassies dispatched to Tang China. China exerted a great influence on the culture and was in turn influenced by the cultures of Korea, India and Persia.

| 1. Heijokyo |
| 2. Buddhhism |
| 3. Heian |
| 4. Taira |
| 5. Genji |

奈良・平安-01-3.

　現在の京都に都が移されたのは8世紀末のことで、こののち1000年以上、ずっと日本の都でしたが、そのうち12世紀末までの約400年間を平安時代といいます。

At the end of the eighth century, the capital was moved to present-day Kyoto, which remained Japan's capital for over 1,000 years. The (　　　　　) period designates a span of roughly 400 years until the 12th century.

1. Heijokyo
2. Buddhhism
3. Heian
4. Taira
5. Genji

奈良・平安-01-4.
　奈良時代に続いて、天皇の下で**貴族**が実権を握って政治を行っていきますが、同時に各地域の**豪族**が次第に**私有地**を拡大し、周辺との争いから身を守るために武装して団結します。そして、ついに平氏という一族が政治の全権を握ります。やがて来る武士の時代のさきがけです。

Continuing from the Nara period, aristocrats under the emperor held actual power and controlled the government; but at the same time, powerful clans from a variety of regions expanded their private landholdings and became unified and militarized in order to protect themselves from war with neighboring regions. Eventually, the (　　　　　) clan was able to grasp full political control. It was a sign of the age of the warrior that was soon to follow.

1. Heijokyo
2. Buddhhism
3. Heian
4. Taira
5. Genji

奈良・平安-01-5.
　文化の面では、唐の文化の**模倣**と**吸収**から脱して、日本の独特の風土や日本人の感性による文化へと移行しました。仮名の発達と仮名文の普及により、世界的に有名な紫式部の「源氏物語」、清少納言の「枕草子」などが生まれたのもこの時代です。

　In the cultural sphere, Japan was able to move away from its reliance on imitating and assimilating Tang culture and proceeded to forge a culture that incorporated a distinct Japanese spirit and sensitivity. Due to the development and spread of hiragana and katakana, world-renowned literary works, such as "Tale of (　　　　)" by Murasaki Shikibu and "Makura no Soshi (The Pillow Book)" by Sei Shonagon were created during this period.

1. Heijokyo
2. Buddhhism
3. Heian
4. Taira
5. Genji

鎌倉-02-1.

平安時代末期に政治の実権を握っていた平氏も、1185年、ついに源氏に滅ぼされます。

The (　　　　　　　) family, which had grasped political power toward the end of the Heian period, was overthrown by the Minamoto family in 1185.

1. Taira
2. shogunate
3. Go-Daigo
4. Zen Buddisim

鎌倉-02-2.

平氏を滅ぼした源頼朝は、鎌倉（神奈川県）に拠点を定め、**守護**と**地頭**を任命して諸国に置き、勢力を固めました。そして、源頼朝は1192年に征夷大将軍となり、鎌倉幕府が成立しました。武家政治の始まりです。幕府は武士の長である将軍が政務をとった**武家政権**です。天皇は単なる**名目的な存在**でした。

After Minamoto no Yoritomo defeated the Taira family, he set up his base in Kamakura (Kanagawa prefecture), and by assigning constables and stewards throughout the country he was able to solidify his power. In 1192, Minamoto no Yoritomo was given the title seii tai shogun (barbarian-subduing generalissimo) and established a bakufu (　　　　　　) government at Kamakura. This was the beginning of warrior clan politics. Bakufu was the name for a military regime in which the head of the warriors, the shogun, controlled political affairs. The emperor was simply a leader in name only.

1. Taira
2. shogunate
3. Go-Daigo
4. Zen Buddisim

鎌倉-02-3.
　しかし、頼朝が亡くなった後、未亡人の北条政子の一族、北条氏が権力を握り、1333年、後醍醐天皇が鎌倉幕府を倒し、天皇政治を復活するまで続きます。
　文化の面では、武士らしい、力強く、剛毅で、そして写実的な**仏教彫刻**に名作が生まれました。

　After Masako Hojo was left a widow at Yoritomo's death, her family, the Hojo clan, took over and remained in power until Emperor (　　　　　) defeated the Kamakura bakufu government in 1333 and effected a restoration of imperial rule.
　In the cultural sphere, the period gave birth to a number of famous realistic Buddhist sculptures noted for being powerful, bold, and warrior-like.

1. Taira
2. shogunate
3. Go-Daigo
4. Zen Buddisim

鎌倉-02-4.

仏教は庶民の信仰を集めるようになり、法然が浄土宗、日蓮が日蓮宗を興すなどしました。禅宗もこの時代に栄えました。

鎌倉時代の出来事として忘れてならないのは、**蒙古の襲来**です。1274年、1284年の2度にわたって、フビライ・ハンの大軍が九州の博多に押し寄せましたが、いずれの時も、運良く大あらしとなり、蒙古の艦隊は退却していきました。

As Buddhism assimilated the faith of the commoners, Honen established Jodoshu and Nichiren established Nichirenshu. (　　　　　　　) also prospered during this period.

One of the more unforgettable narratives of the Kamakura period was of the Mongolian invasions. In the years 1274 and 1284, the forces of Kublai Khan attempted to invade Kyushu at Hakata, but at both times the Mongolian troops were defeated with the help of large storms at sea.

1. Taira
2. shogunate
3. Go-Daigo
4. Zen Buddisim

室町-03-1.

室町時代は2つに分けられます。**南北朝時代**と**戦国時代**です。

The Muromachi period can be divided into two periods : the Northern and Southern Courts period and the (　　　　　　　) States period.

1. Warring
2. Muromachi
3. Ashikaga
4. Onin
5. Christianity

室町-03-2.

南北朝時代は、1333年に足利尊氏の力で鎌倉幕府を倒し、政権を京都の朝廷に取り戻した後醍醐天皇と、これに背いて、光明天皇をかついで、1336年に京都北部の室町に幕府を開いた足利尊氏とが対立していた時代です。

The Northern and Southern Courts period was the time of conflict between Emperor Go-Daigo, who had overthrown the Kamakura bakufu in 1333 and restored political power to the palace in Kyoto, and Ashikaga Takauji, who set up a bakufu government in (　　　　　) in northern Kyoto under the Emperor Komyo in 1336.

1. Warring
2. Muromachi
3. Ashikaga
4. Onin
5. Christianity

室町-03-3.

　後醍醐天皇の没後は、足利一族による鎌倉幕府が全国支配に乗り出しますが、幕府の力は弱く、諸国には自ら武力を持った守護大名の勢力が高まってきました。1467 年、将軍家の相続問題から、10 年におよぶ応仁の乱が起こり、幕府の権威は失われ、群雄割拠の戦国時代となります。

　After the death of Emperor Go-Daigo, the (　　　　　　　) clan of the Muromachi bakufu set out to rule the entire country, but the power of the bakufu weakened while the power of the Shugo daimyo throughout the country increased. In 1467, problems of succession in shogun families marked the Onin War that lasted ten years. And as the bakufu lost power, the country entered the Warring States period of fighting and disorder.

1. Warring
2. Muromachi
3. Ashikaga
4. Onin
5. Christianity

室町-03-4.

　戦国時代は、1467 年の応仁の乱以後、1573 年に織田信長が幕府を滅ぼすまでの約 100 年間です。

　The Warring States period is the 100-year period beginning with the (　　　　　　　) War in 1467 and continuing until Oda Nobunaga's defeat of the bakufu in 1573.

| 1. Warring |
| 2. Muromachi |
| 3. Ashikaga |
| 4. Onin |
| 5. Christianity |

室町-03-5.

　室町時代には、全般的には、農業生産が向上し、商業も発展し、都市が栄えました。

　文化面でも**水墨画**、能、狂言、**茶の湯**、生け花などがこの時代に広まりました。**キリスト教**もまた、1549年のフランシスコ・ザビエルの来日によって、日本に伝えられました。

　Overall, the Muromachi period saw the rise of agricultural production, the growth of commercial activity, and the development of cities.

　Culturally, this period witnessed the birth of ink painting, no and kyogen theater, the tea ceremony, and Japanese flower arrangement. And with the arrival of Francisco Xavier in 1549, (　　　　　) was brought to Japan.

| 1. Warring |
| 2. Muromachi |
| 3. Ashikaga |
| 4. Onin |
| 5. Christianity |

安土桃山-04-1.

戦国時代にライバルを次々と倒していったのが織田信長でした。しかし彼は、**全国統一**を目前にして**家臣**の明智光秀に殺されてしまいました。その後を引き継いだのが、やはり家臣だった豊臣秀吉でした。安土桃山時代はこの織田信長と豊臣秀吉が政権を握っていた時代です。1568 年（1573 年説もある）から約 30 年という短期間ですが、日本の**封建制度**を発展させた点で重要な時代です。

During the (　　　　　　　) States period, Oda Nobunaga went on to defeat one rival after another. However, just before he could achieve unification of the country, he was killed by his own vassal, Akechi Mitsuhide. The person who succeeded him was another of his subjects, Toyotomi Hideyoshi. Azuchi-Momoyama covers the period when political control was held by Oda Nobunaga and Toyotomi Hideyoshi. The short, roughly 30-year span beginning in 1568 (some say 1573) was a crucial period in terms of the development of Japan's feudal society.

1. Warring
2. the sword hunt
3. Momoyama

安土桃山-04-2.

注目すべき 2 つの政策は**検地**と**刀狩り**です。農地面積や収穫高などを調べ、年貢の量と責任者を決める検地、そして、農民から一切の武器を取りあげる刀狩りは、農民の身分を固定化し、武士の支配的地位を決定づけました。

The two policies which deserve attention are the cadastral survey and (   ). The former, which estimated the area and productivity of agricultural land, and the latter, which seized all weaponry held by peasants, served to establish the domination of the warrior class and entrench the status of the peasant.

1. Warring
2. the sword hunt
3. Momoyama

安土桃山-04-3.
　文化は桃山文化と呼ばれ、仏教の影響が弱まり、自由で豪華な様相を呈しました。高くそびえる天守閣を持つ城郭建築や金箔にきらめく**障壁画**がその典型です。

In terms of culture, this period gave rise to what is known as the (   ) culture, which saw the weakening of Buddhist influence and the emergence of a free and luxurious style. Typifying this culture were the building of castles with soaring towers and the creation of wall and screen paintings glittering with gold leaf.

1. Warring
2. the sword hunt
3. Momoyama

江戸-05-1.
豊臣家を滅ぼし、1603年、徳川家康が江戸（東京）に幕府を開いて全国を支配した260年余が江戸時代です。

The Edo period is the 260-year span following Tokugawa Ieyasu's defeat of the (　　　　　　) family and the establishment of a bakufu government in Edo (now Tokyo) in 1603.

1. Toyotomi
2. bakuhan
3. Christianity
4. Genroku

江戸-05-2.
幕府の**最高権力者**、将軍から1万石以上の領地を得た者が大名で、その**領地**と支配機構を藩といいます。幕府はこの藩を通して全国の領土と民衆を支配します。この支配体制が幕藩制です。

The daimyo ranged from the shogun, who sat at the top of power, to lords controlling land worth over 10,000 koku (a unit of measure based on rice production), and their domains and the power structure imposed on them were known as han. The bakufu controlled the land and the people of the nation through these han units. This system of government is known as the (　　　　　　) system.

1. Toyotomi
2. bakuhan
3. Christianity
4. Genroku

江戸-05-3.
　武士をいちばん上の階級とする士農工商の制度で身分差別を強め、対外的には、**鎖国政策**をとり、キリスト教を禁じた時代でもあります。

　This period also saw the reinforcement of a status system known as shi-no-ko-sho (worrior-peasant-artisan-merchant), which placed the warrior in the top social class, and externally, the establishment of a policy of national seclusion and the prohibition of (　　　　　).

1. Toyotomi
2. bakuhan
3. Christianity
4. Genroku

江戸-05-4.
　しかし、国内の作物の栽培は進み、漁業も発達し、商人が力をつけて、**貨幣経済**が発展しました。
　文化の面では、17世紀末〜18世紀初めに元禄文化が花開きます。町民が担い手で、**人形浄瑠璃**や歌舞伎が人気を博し、松尾芭蕉が俳句を大成しました。浮世絵が創始され、歌麿、北斎、広重ら多くの浮世絵師が出ました。

However, during this period, advances were made in domestic agricultural production as well as in fishing industries, which strengthened the merchant class and gave rise to a monetary economy.

Culturally, this period saw the flourishing in the latter 17th and early 18th centuries of what is known as the (　　　　　) culture. Fostered by the townspeople, arts such as the puppet theater and kabuki gained popularity, while Matsuo Basho produced masterpieces in the haiku poetic form. The art of ukiyo-e prints which was fostered by Utamaro, Hokusai, Hiroshige and many other artists, also began during this period.

1. Toyotomi
2. bakuhan
3. Christianity
4. Genroku

明治-06-1.
1853年、ペリー率いるアメリカ軍艦が浦賀沖に現れ開国を迫るや、国内は開国か**尊皇攘夷**かを巡って大混乱に陥りました。倒幕の主力ともなった薩摩藩（鹿児島県）と長州藩（山口県）も、当初は尊皇攘夷でしたが、欧米の力を知るに至って**開国**へと方向転換します。

In 1853, Commodore Perry and his squadron of American ships appeared in Uraga Bay to press for the opening of the country, leaving in their wake a domestic crisis over whether to open up or "worship the emperor and expel the barbarians." Even Satsuma (now Kagoshima prefecture) and (　　　　　　　) provinces (now Yamaguchi prefecture), which eventually overthrew the bakufu, initially supported the move to "worship the emperor and expel the barbarians," but eventually, with their growing knowledge of the Western power, they decided to switch their allegiance toward the drive to open up the country.

---

1. Choshu
2. Yoshinobu
3. the Meiji Constitution
4. the Sino-Japanese War

明治-06-2.

　一方、民衆は**物価上昇**に苦しみ、富裕な商店を襲う打ち壊しや一揆が各地で続発、ここからも幕藩制の根底が揺るぎました。ついに15代将軍、徳川慶喜は、1867年、政権を朝廷に返します。そして天皇中心の政府を樹立する王政復古の大号令が出され、長い**封建制度**は終わりを告げます。明治時代の誕生です。

　On one hand, the masses were suffering under inflation, and riots and attacks on shops of wealthy merchants occurred in various regions, weakening the foundations of the bakuhan system. This led in 1867 to the relinquishing of power by the 15th Tokugawa shogun, (　　　　　　　　　　), to the Imperial Court. A decree was made which established a government centered around the emperor, bringing to a close the long-lasting feudal system. This is how the Meiji period came into being.

1. Choshu
2. Yoshinobu
3. the Meiji Constitution
4. the Sino-Japanese War

明治-06-3.

　徳川氏から**朝廷**へと政権が移行し、幕府と藩による政治から国家統一に向かうことになりました。経済は資本主義制度へと移行して、近代日本の制度ができた時代です。

　1889年、明治憲法（大日本帝国憲法）が発布されて、国の政治形態の基本ができますが、「天皇は神聖にて侵すべからず」という条項があり、天皇は神格化され、日本は次第に**国家主義**で統一されていきます。

This period saw the transfer of power from Tokugawa to the Imperial Court, and the transition from a system of government based on the bakufu and han domains to a unified state. This was also the period that witnessed the transition to a capitalist economy and the establishment of a modern Japanese state system.

In 1889, (　　　　　　　　　　) (the Constitution of Imperial Japan) was promulgated, laying the foundation for the political structure of the state. It contained a clause maintaining the divinity of the emperor, proclaiming that the country "must not violate the holiness of the emperor," and thus Japan gradually became unified under the force of nationalism.

1. Choshu
2. Yoshinobu
3. the Meiji Constitution
4. the Sino-Japanese War

明治-06-4.

　これに対して、人民の自由と権利を伸ばすことを主張する**自由民権運動**が起こりますが、結局は、**国家主義の名のもとに**、国益が優先され、朝鮮半島、中国大陸への進出をします。そしてこれに反対する諸外国との**軋轢**も強まり、明治時代だけで、**日清戦争**（1894-95）、**日露戦争**（1904-05）に突入し、1910年には韓国を日本に**合併する**という事態になっていきました。

　In protest against nationalism, human rights movements arose to assert and extend the rights and freedom of citizens.　But in the end, under the banner of nationalism, Japan let state interests take precedence and advanced into the Korean peninsula and the Chinese continent.　Friction increased with countries that opposed Japan's advances, and in the Meiji period alone, Japan entered into (　　　　　　　　　　) (1894-1895) and the Russo-Japanese War (1904-1905), and went on to annex Korea in 1910.

1. Choshu
2. Yoshinobu
3. the Meiji Constitution
4. the Sino-Japanese War

大正-07-1.

この時代には 1912 年から 26 年までの 14 年間という短い期間ですが、明治時代の藩閥・官僚政治による国家権力の増大に反発して、憲法にのっとった政治を守ること、誰でもが**選挙権**を持つことができる**普通選挙**を求める運動などが繰り広げられます。

This was a short 14-year period from 1912 to 1926, which saw opposition to growing state power in the hands of the han bureaucratic clique from the Meiji period. There was a spread of popular movements which demanded that government abide by the constitution and called for common elections which extended (　　　　　　) to all citizens.

1. voting rights
2. Taisho Democracy
3. educational reforms

大正-07-2.

米騒動や**労働争議**も起こり、民本主義、自由主義、社会主義の運動が高まった時代です。この運動を「大正デモクラシー」と呼んでいます。

しかしこの運動も、結局、高まる国家主義の動きに抗することはできず、日本は次第に**軍国主義の国**になっていきます。

This was a period when rice riots and labor disputes occurred, and democratic and socialist movements were heightened. Such movements are referred to as (　　　　　　).

However, even these movements in the end could not stop rising nationalism, and Japan would increasingly turn into a militarist state.

1. voting rights
2. Taisho Democracy
3. educational reforms

昭和-08-1.
　日露戦争後、日本は**満州**における権益の確保政策を続け、大陸に駐留する関東軍は満州占領を進めて、1932年には「満州建国宣言」をします。
　これに異議をとなえる**国際連盟**は**調査団**を送りますが、日本は国際連盟を脱退しまいます。

　After the Russo-Japanese War, Japan continued its policy of extending power in Manchuria, and the Kwantung Army stationed on the continent furthered its occupation of Manchuria, and in 1932 issued the "Declaration of the Founding of Manchukuo."
　In protest, (　　　　　　　　　　) sent an investigative commission to Manchuria, while Japan withdrew from the League.

1. the League of Nations
2. attack on Pearl Harbor
3. allied forces
4. Article 9 of the Constitution
5. the United States-Japan Security Treaty
6. the Korean War
7. the Liberal-Democratic Party
8. the economic "bubble"

昭和-08-2.

さらに1937年、深夜演習中の日本軍と中国軍が衝突するという**盧溝橋事件**を契機に中国との間に戦争となり、ついには、東南アジア一帯にも日本が介入するにおよび、1941年12月8日の真珠湾攻撃を開始の合図に、日本はアメリカその他の国々との**全面戦争**に突入しました。

結果は、1945年8月、日本は敗戦となります。

In 1937, propelled by the Marco Polo Bridge Incident when Japanese forces on night training clashed with Chinese troops, Japan entered into a war with China, and soon it intervened in all of Southeast Asia. Japan's (　　　　　　　　　　) on December 8, 1941, signaled its thrust into full-scale war with the United States and other countries.

In the end, Japan was defeated in August 1945.

1. the League of Nations
2. attack on Pearl Harbor
3. allied forces
4. Article 9 of the Constitution
5. the United States-Japan Security Treaty
6. the Korean War
7. the Liberal-Democratic Party
8. the economic "bubble"

昭和-08-3.
　敗戦の結果、日本は**連合軍**の占領下におかれることになり、新しい日本国憲法の制定、農地改革、教育革命、財閥の解体、日本の伝統的な家制度の廃止などの改革が進められました。

　After Japan was defeated, the country was placed under the (　　　　　　　　　　　　　　), while reforms that included the creation of a new constitution, agrarian and educational reforms, dissolution of zaibatsu (financial cliques), and abolition of the Japanese traditional family system were carried out.

---

1. the League of Nations
2. attack on Pearl Harbor
3. allied forces
4. Article 9 of the Constitution
5. the United States-Japan Security Treaty
6. the Korean War
7. the Liberal-Democratic Party
8. the economic "bubble"

昭和-08-4.
　新憲法では、国民が国の主権者であることが明記され、天皇は国の象徴とされました。のちに**自衛隊**が誕生しますが、**憲法第９条**には軍備の放棄がうたわれました。農地改革では**小作制度**が廃止され、地主が所有していた農地の多くは農民に開放されました。教育革命では**男女共学**になり、小学校の６年間、中学校の３年間の義務教育が定められました。また、家制度の廃止で、子供を**家への従属**から開放し、核家族の誕生、女性の自由な恋愛などへの道が開かれていきました。

The new Constitution ruled that sovereignty lies with the citizens and that the emperor serves as a symbol of the nation. (   ) forbids Japan from possessing arms, although a self-defense force was later formed. Under agrarian reform, the tenant farmer system was abolished and the farms held by landlords were distributed to the farmers. With educational reform, a coeducational system was inspired and six years of elementary school and three years of junior high school were made compulsory. The abolition of the family system freed children from the old clan bondage, nuclear families became the norm, and women obtained the freedom to choose marriage partners.

1. the League of Nations
2. attack on Pearl Harbor
3. allied forces
4. Article 9 of the Constitution
5. the United States-Japan Security Treaty
6. the Korean War
7. the Liberal-Democratic Party
8. the economic "bubble"

昭和-08-5.
　1951年6月に日本は、共産圏を除く48カ国との間にサンフランシスコ講和条約を締結し、占領体制は終わり、同時に、アメリカとの間に日米安全保障条約を締結しました。

In June 1951, Japan signed the San Francisco Peace Treaty with 48 countries, none of which were from the Communist bloc, thus leading to the end of allied occupation.　At this same time, Japan also concluded (　　　　　　　　　　).

---

1. the League of Nations
2. attack on Pearl Harbor
3. allied forces
4. Article 9 of the Constitution
5. the United States-Japan Security Treaty
6. the Korean War
7. the Liberal-Democratic Party
8. the economic "bubble"

昭和-08-6.

戦後の経済復興には困難が伴いましたが、アメリカの支援、1 ドルが 360 円という安定した**為替相場**、また、1950 年におこった朝鮮戦争の際の軍事需要などの景気で、日本の経済力は強まり、1955 年から 60 年にかけて、日本の国民総生産は毎年 9%以上の伸びを見せていました。

Japan's postwar economic rehabilitation has involved difficulties, but the Japanese economy became stronger with America's support, a stable exchange rate of 360 yen to the dollar, and the prosperity resulting from the war boom during (　　　　　　　　　　) in the 1950s. The GNP (Gross National Product) of Japan grew nine percent every year from 1955 to 1960.

1. the League of Nations
2. attack on Pearl Harbor
3. allied forces
4. Article 9 of the Constitution
5. the United States-Japan Security Treaty
6. the Korean War
7. the Liberal-Democratic Party
8. the economic "bubble"

昭和-08-7.

　高度な工業技術によって船舶、テレビ、自動車など、多くの製品の主要な生産国になり、1970年代、1980年代には輸出が増大しました。それに対して海外から輸出規制の圧力が高まりましたが、日本の貿易収支はとりわけアメリカに対して、大幅な黒字を続けました。

　政治は、**自民党**がほぼ独占に権力を握り続けましたが、経済の**高度成長**にはいろいろなひずみも生じ、様々な公害や環境破壊などを生んでいきました。

　文化的には、あらゆる面でアメリカ、ヨーロッパの**流行**が取り入れられ、特に若者を中心に一気に西欧化したのもこの時代です。

　Due to a high level of engineering skill, Japan became a major exporter of various products such as ships, televisions, and automobiles, and in the 1970s and 1980s Japanese exports rose sharply. Pressure from abroad to exercise self-restraint in exports mounted, but Japan's trade surplus kept rising, especially with the United States.

　As for politics, (　　　　　　　　　　　) has maintained a monopolistic grip on power, but the high economic growth rate has brought about various problems, such as pollution and the destruction of the environment.

And culturally, this was a period when all sorts of fashions from America and Europe were introduced, and almost overnight the country became westernized.

---

1. the League of Nations
2. attack on Pearl Harbor
3. allied forces
4. Article 9 of the Constitution
5. the United States-Japan Security Treaty
6. the Korean War
7. the Liberal-Democratic Party
8. the economic "bubble"

昭和-08-8.

そして好景気にあおられて、1986年、いわゆるバブル経済が始まります。異常な地価の高騰に日本中が浮かれる中、1989年1月、昭和天皇が亡くなられ、時代は平成に移ることになりました。

Powered by the strong economy, (   ) began to form in 1986. Land prices rose to unreasonable levels and, with the country in a state of euphoria, Emperor Showa passed away in January 1989, making room for the new Heisei period.

1. the League of Nations
2. attack on Pearl Harbor
3. allied forces
4. Article 9 of the Constitution
5. the United States-Japan Security Treaty
6. the Korean War
7. the Liberal-Democratic Party
8. the economic "bubble"

第5章

英作文 ―条件英作文―

「第5章 英作文 ―条件英作文―」では、英作文をする上で重要な内容を学習しましょう。「考えるべき事柄」と「その解答」をセットで述べる形式で進んでいます。

問題
・教会を通りかかった時にウエディングドレス姿の花嫁さんを見た外国からの訪問者に、「日本にはクリスチャンが多いのですか。」と質問されました。あなたならどう答えますか。日本人の信仰心、ならびに現在の一般的な結婚式事情なども含めて、英語で書きなさい。語数は特に指定しない。

・条件英作文を書くポイントは？
1. 文法の間違いを減らし、多くの文法事項を使う。

2. 求められている情報を多く書き、それ以外はできるだけ書かない。

3. メリハリのある文章を書く。

・条件英作文を書くポイントは？
1. 文法の間違いを減らし、多くの文法事項を使う。
　　①関係代名詞・関係副詞、②従属接続詞を使う。

2. 求められている情報を多く書き、それ以外はできるだけ書かない。
　　<u>①名詞、②動詞、③形容詞の語彙を増やす。</u>

3. メリハリのある文章を書く。
　　<u>序論(起)、本論(承・転)、結論(結)を目指す。</u>

・条件英作文を書くポイントは？
1. ①関係代名詞・関係副詞の使用総語数(省略を含む)は？　　＿＿＿語
　　②従属接続詞の使用総語数は？　　　　　　　　　　　　＿＿＿語

2. 使用総語数は？　　　　　　　　　　＿＿＿語（無制限＝約 150 語）
　　使用実質語数は？　　　　　　　　　　　　　　　　　　＿＿＿語
　　①名詞の使用実質語数は？　　　　　　　　　　　　　　＿＿＿語
　　②動詞の使用実質語数は？　　　　　　　　　　　　　　＿＿＿語
　　③形容詞の使用実質語数は？　　　　　　　　　　　　　＿＿＿語

3. 序論(起)、本論(承・転)、結論(結)の使用はあるか？

・接続詞とは？

	等位接続詞	従属接続詞	機能
1	and		原因―結果
2	so		原因―結果
3	or		並立
4	but		対立
5	for（というのは）		原因―結果

重文：単文＋，等位接続詞＋単文

　　⇒　複文：

　　※　文 ≒ 節 ≒ 主語 ＋ (述語)動詞 ～

・接続詞とは？

	等位接続詞	従属接続詞	機能
1	and	when（～の時）	原因―結果
2	so	that（～ということ）	原因―結果
3	or	if	並立
4	but	though（although）	対立
5	for（というのは）	because（as, since）	原因―結果

重文：単文＋，等位接続詞＋単文

　　⇒　複文：主節＋従属接続詞＋従属節／

　　　　　　従属接続詞＋従属接，主節

　　※　文 ≒ 節 ≒ 主語 ＋ (述語)動詞 ～

・解答例（学生１）

　There aren't so many Chrischan in Japan.

　Japanese people have some culture which is from a lot of countries, and don't care about one religion.

We also have many events such as Chrismas, Valent Day, Hinamatsuri and so on.

　On the other hand, when we have marriage, we often put on both kimono and wedding-dress.

　This is why Japanese people have diverse religion custom.

・条件英作文を書くポイントは？
1. ①関係代名詞・関係副詞の使用総語数（省略を含む）は？
　　　　　　　　　　　　　　　　　　　　　　　　　　　＿＿＿語
　　②従属接続詞の使用総語数は？　　　　　　　　　　　＿＿＿語

2. 使用総語数は？　　　　　　　　　＿＿＿語（無制限=約 150 語）
　　使用実質語数は？　　　　　　　　　　　　　　　　　＿＿＿語
　　　①名詞の使用実質語数は？　　　　　　　　　　　　＿＿＿語
　　　②動詞の使用実質語数は？　　　　　　　　　　　　＿＿＿語
　　　③形容詞の使用実質語数は？　　　　　　　　　　　＿＿＿語

3. 序論(起)、本論(承・転)、結論(結)の使用はあるか？

・解答例（学生１）の分析
　There aren't so many Chrischan in Japan.
　Japanese people have some culture **which**（関・代）is from a lot of countries, and don't care about one religion.
　We also have many events such as Chrismas, Valent Day, Hinamatsuri and so on.

On the other hand, **when（従・接）** we have marriage, we often put on both kimono and wedding-dress.

　This is **why（関・副）** Japanese people have diverse religion custom.

・条件英作文を書くポイントは？
1. ①関係代名詞・関係副詞の使用総語数(省略を含む)は？
　　　　　　　　　　　　　　　　　　　　　　　　　　__2_ 語
　　②従属接続詞の使用総語数は？　　　　　　　　　　__1_ 語

2. 使用総語数は？　　　　　　　__64__語（無制限 ＝ 約150語）
　　使用実質語数は？　　　　　　　　　　　　　　　　__49_ 語
　　　①名詞の使用実質語数は？　　　　　　　　　　　__16_ 語
　　　②動詞の使用実質語数は？　　　　　　　　　　　__5_ 語
　　　③形容詞の使用実質語数は？　　　　　　　　　　__7_ 語

3. 序論（起）、本論（承・転）、結論（結）の使用はあるか？
　　→　　ある

・解答例（学生１）の修正
　　There aren't so many ~~Chrischan~~ in Japan.
　　　→　　　　　　　　　Christians

　　Japanese people have some ~~culture~~ which ~~is~~ from a lot of
　　　→　　　　　　　　　　　　cultures　　　are

countries, ~~and don't~~ care about one religion.
→   and Japanese people don't

We also have many ~~events~~
→   events (which are) related to various religions,

~~such as Chrismas, Valent Day~~,
→   such as Christmas and St. Valentine's Day for Christianity,

~~Hinamatsuri and so on~~
→   obon: a three-day Buddhist holiday for Buddhism.

~~On the other hand~~, when we ~~have marriage~~, we often put on
→   Similarly,   get married

~~both kimono and wedding-dress~~.
→   both traditional Japanese cloth<u>es</u>, such as kimonos and western-style clothes, such as wedding dress<u>es</u> / both traditional Japanese <u>clothing,</u> such as a kimono and western-style <u>clothing</u>, such as <u>a</u> wedding dress.

~~This is why~~ Japanese people have diverse ~~religion custom~~.
→   **(In) this way,**   religious customs including weddings.

・解答例（学生１）の修正の分析

（日本にはクリスチャンが多いのですか。→）There aren't so many Christians in Japan.（日本人の信仰心 →）Japanese people have some cultures **which**（関・代）are from a lot of countries, and Japanese people don't care about one religion.

We also have many events **which**（関・代）are related to various religions, such as Christmas and St. Valentine's Day for Christianity, obon: a three-day Buddhist holiday for Buddhism.

（現在の一般的な結婚式事情 →）Similarly, **when**（従・接）we get married, we often put on both traditional Japanese clothes, such as kimonos, and western-style clothes, such as wedding dresses.

In this way, Japanese people have diverse religious customs including weddings.

・条件英作文を書くポイントは？
1. ①関係代名詞・関係副詞の使用総語数（省略を含む）は？
   　　　　　　　　　　　　　　　　　　　　　　　2 → 2 語
   ②従属接続詞の使用総語数は？　　　　　　　　　　**1 → 1** 語

2. 使用総語数は？　　　　　**64 → 90** 語（無制限＝約 150 語）
   使用実質語数は？　　　　　　　　　　　　　　**49 → 65** 語
   　①名詞の使用実質語数は？　　　　　　　　　　**16 → 21** 語
   　②動詞の使用実質語数は？　　　　　　　　　　**5 → 6** 語
   　③形容詞の使用実質語数は？　　　　　　　　　**7 → 13** 語

3. 序論（起）、本論（承・転）、結論（結）の使用はあるか？
   　→　ある

・解答例（学生２）

I do not think that there are many Christians in Japan. In fact, the number of Christian people in Japan is less than 1% of the whole population.

Therefore, it is not because people want a "Christian" wedding that they get married in a wedding chapel with a "priest." Rather, perhaps it is the appeal of the Western style of wedding that draws people to wedding chapels: the regal white gown, the expectant groom at the end of the aisle, and the abundance of fragrant flowers. The Japanese culture is one of rich heritageand rituals, so it may seem to an onlooker, that this popular style of wedding ceremony stems from adherence to orthodox Christian theology and doctrine.

However, given that Japan remains a very unchristianized country, the more likely conclusion is that it is the outward draw of the traditional Christian wedding that intrigues Japanese brides-to-be rather than the Christian approach to the marriage itself.

・条件英作文を書くポイントは？
1. ①関係代名詞・関係副詞の使用総語数（省略を含む）は？
　　　　　　　　　　　　　　　　　　　　　　　　____語
　　②従属接続詞の使用総語数は？　　　　　　　　____語

2. 使用総語数は？　　　　　　____語（無制限＝約 150 語）

使用実質語数は？　　　　　　　　　　　　＿＿語
　　　①名詞の使用実質語数は？　　　　　　　　　＿＿語
　　　②動詞の使用実質語数は？　　　　　　　　　＿＿語
　　　③形容詞の使用実質語数は？　　　　　　　　＿＿語

3. 序論（起）、本論（承・転）、結論（結）の使用はあるか？

・解答例（学生２）の分析

　I do not think **that**（従・接）there are many Christians in Japan. In fact, the number of Christian people in Japan is less than 1% of the whole population.

　Therefore, it is not **because**（従・接）people want a "Christian" wedding **that**（関・副）they get married in a wedding chapel with a "priest." Rather, perhaps it is the appeal of the Western style of wedding **that**（関・代）draws people to wedding chapels: the regal white gown, the expectant groom at the end of the aisle, and the abundance of fragrant flowers. The Japanese culture is one of rich heritage and rituals, so it may seem to an onlooker, **that** （従・接）this popular style of wedding ceremony stems from adherence to orthodox Christian theology and doctrine.

　However, given **that**（従・接）Japan remains a very unchristianized country, the more likely conclusion is **that**（従・接）it is the outward draw of the traditional Christian wedding **that**（関・代）intrigues Japanese brides-to-be rather than the Christian approach to the marriage itself.

第5章　英作文　—条件英作文—

・条件英作文を書くポイントは？

1. ①関係代名詞・関係副詞の使用総語数（省略を含む）は？
   <u>**3**</u> 語

   ②従属接続詞の使用総語数は？
   <u>**5**</u> 語

2. 使用総語数は？　　<u>**158**</u> 語（無制限＝約 150 語）
   使用実質語数は？　　　　　　　　　　　　<u>**90**</u> 語
   ①名詞の使用実質語数は？　　　　　　　　<u>**32**</u> 語
   ②動詞の使用実質語数は？　　　　　　　　<u>**10**</u> 語
   ③形容詞の使用実質語数は？　　　　　　　<u>**16**</u> 語

3. 序論（起）、本論（承・転）、結論（結）の使用はあるか？
   →　**ある**

・第1解答者と第2解答者の形式比較

項目		使用語数	第1解答者	第2解答者
1	①	関係代名詞・関係副詞の使用総語数	2 → 2	3
	②	従属接続詞の使用総語数	1 → 1	5
2		使用総語数	64 → 90	158
		使用実質語数	49 → 65	90
	※	文の数	5 → 5	6
	①	名詞の使用実質語数	16 → 21	32
	②	動詞の使用実質語数	5 → 6	10
	③	形容詞の使用実質語数	7 → 13	16
3		序論、本論、結論（起承転結）	ある	ある

・解答例（学生2）の分析（内容）
(日本にはクリスチャンが多いのですか。→) I do not think **that** (従・接) there are many Christians in Japan.

(日本人の信仰心 →) In fact, the number of Christian people in Japan is less than 1% of the whole population.

(現在の一般的な結婚式事情 →) Therefore, it is not **because**（従・接) people want a "Christian" wedding **that** (関・副) they get married in a wedding chapel with a "priest." Rather, perhaps it is the appeal of the Western style of wedding **that** (関・代) draws people to wedding chapels: the regal white gown, the expectant groom at the end of the aisle, and the abundance of fragrant flowers. The Japanese culture is one of rich heritage and rituals, so it may seem to an onlooker, **that** (従・接) this popular style of wedding ceremony stems from adherence to orthodox Christian theology and doctrine.

However, given **that** (従・接) Japan remains a very unchristianized country, the more likely conclusion is **that** (従・接) it is the outward draw of the traditional Christian wedding **that**) (関・代) intrigues Japanese brides-to-be rather than the Christian approach to the marriage itself.

第1解答者と第2解答者の内容比較

項目	ポイント	第1解答者	第2解答者
1	日本のクリスチャンの数	○	○
2	日本人の信仰心	△（具体的に宗教に触れていない。） ○	△（説明が少ない。仏教や神道の記述がない。）
3	日本の結婚式事情	△（説明が少ない。） △（具体的に宗教に触れていない。）	○（キリスト教に関してはとても良いが、神前結婚の記述がない。）
総合	―	4点 5点	5点

◎3点　　○2点　　△1点　　6点満点（0点 〜 9点）
2段の表示は修正前と修正後

課題

・教会を通りかかった時にウエディングドレス姿の花嫁さんを見た外国からの訪問者に、「日本にはクリスチャンが多いのですか。」と質問されました。あなたならどう答えますか。日本人の信仰心、ならびに現在の一般的な結婚式事情なども含めて、英語で書きなさい。語数は特に指定しない。

第6章

日本事情 —英単語 & 英文説明—

「第6章 日本事情 —英単語 & 英文説明—」では、日本の文化を紹介する上で、重要な英単語と英文を学習しましょう。

日本の文化に関する、項目別の英語を理解し、英語で言えるようにしよう！

日本事情 —英単語—

番号	項目
1	地理・歴史
2	旅行・観光
3	食事・料理
4	芸術・音楽
5	スポーツ・娯楽
6	宗教
7	文化行事
8	生活様式・体・病気
9	教育・ビジネス
10	日本人

日本事情 —英単語—

番号	項目
1	active volcano　活火山, ideogram　表意文字, paddy field　水田
2	customs clearance　通関手続き, donjon　天守閣, itinerary　旅行日程
3	cuisine　料理（法）, ingredient　（料理の）材料, soy sauce　しょう油
4	ballad　民謡, fine arts　美術品, hanging scroll　掛け軸
5	loincloth　ふんどし, martial arts　武道, (the art of) self-defense　護身術
6	Confucianism　儒教, funeral　葬式, Shinto priest　神主
7	emperor　天皇, evil spirit　悪霊, nobility　貴族
8	alcove　床の間, family crest　家紋, fatigue　疲労
9	calligraphy　書道, cram school　塾, grocery　食料雑貨店
10	flattery　お世辞, human feelings　人情, social obligation　義理

日本の文化に関する、項目別の英語の説明（対）を理解し、英語で言えるようにしよう！

日本事情　―英文説明―

番号	項目
1	地理・歴史
2	旅行・観光
3	食事・料理
4	芸術・音楽
5	スポーツ・娯楽
6	宗教
7	文化行事
8	生活様式・体・病気
9	教育・ビジネス
10	日本人

寺と神社（6．宗教）

・*Tera* is a Buddhist temple where funerals, memorial services, and other events are conducted.　*Jinja* is a Shinto shrine where a particular *kami*, Shinto deity is enshrined.　Shinto is the indigenous religion of Japan.　People visit *jinja* to make wedding vows, celebrate births and the New Year, and make prayers.　Many *jinja* and *tera* are popular tourist attractions especially in Kyoto and Nara.

寺と神社（6．宗教）

・*Tera* is a Buddhist temple where funerals, memorial services, and other events are conducted. *Jinja* is a Shinto shrine where a particular *kami*, Shinto deity is enshrined. Shinto is the indigenous religion of Japan. People visit *jinja* to make wedding vows, celebrate births and the New Year, and make prayers. Many *jinja* and *tera* are popular tourist attractions especially in Kyoto and Nara.

お盆と正月（7．文化行事）

・*Obon* is a three-day Buddhist holiday, usually on August 13, 14, and 15. During this time the spirits of the dead are said to return to their former homes and families. The week of *obon* is considered *bon-yasumi*, or *bon* vacation, and many people return to their hometowns or take trips. *Shogatsu* is the celebration of the New Year and is the most important holiday in Japan, comparable to Christmas in Western countries.

お盆と正月（7．文化行事）

・*Obon* is a three-day Buddhist holiday, usually on August 13, 14, and 15. During this time the spirits of the dead are said to return to their former homes and families. The week of *obon* is considered *bon-yasumi*, or *bon* vacation, and many people return to their hometowns or take trips. *Shogatsu* is the celebration of the New Year and is the most important holiday in Japan, comparable to Christmas in Western countries.

着物と浴衣（8．生活様式・体・病気）
- A kimono is the long robe with wide sleeves and a broad sash which is traditionally worn as an outer garment by Japanese people. *Yukata* is a light cotton kimono for summer wear. It is also commonly worn at some summer events, such as local festivals and fireworks display.

着物と浴衣（8．生活様式・体・病気）
- A kimono is <u>the long robe with wide sleeves and a broad sash</u> which is traditionally worn as <u>an outer garment</u> by Japanese people. *Yukata* is <u>a light cotton kimono for summer wear.</u> It is also commonly worn at some summer events, such as <u>local festivals and fireworks display.</u>

漢字とひらがな（9．教育・ビジネス）
- *Kanji* are the Chinese characters on which the Japanese writing system is based. Each *kanji* is a symbol for a concept and is used for writing content words or root elements. *Hiragana* are cursive phonetic characters simplified from *kanji*. They are mainly used in combination with *kanji*.

漢字とひらがな（9．教育・ビジネス）
- *Kanji* are <u>the Chinese characters on which the Japanese writing system is based.</u> Each *kanji* is a symbol for <u>a concept</u> and is used for writing <u>content words or root elements.</u> *Hiragana* are <u>cursive phonetic characters simplified from *kanji*.</u> They are

94

mainly used in combination with *kanji*.

本音と建前（10. 日本人）

・*Honne* refers to one's true feelings or motives, whereas *tatemae* is the face one wears in public. *Honne* may be expressed privately, while *tatemae* are opinions designed for social acceptance. Japanese people are group-conscious, so it is very important to use both *tatemae* and *honne* properly in Japanese society especially in a company.

本音と建前（10. 日本人）

・*Honne* refers to one's true feelings or motives, whereas *tatemae* is the face one wears in public. *Honne* may be expressed privately, while *tatemae* are opinions designed for social acceptance. Japanese people are group-conscious, so it is very important to use both *tatemae* and *honne* properly in Japanese society especially in a company.

日本事情 —英文説明（6〜10）—

番号	事象	重要語句
6	寺（と）	Buddhist temple
	神社	Shinto shrine
7	お盆（と）	a three-day Buddhist holiday
	正月	the celebration of the New Year
8	着物（と）	a long robe with wide sleeves and a broad sash
	浴衣	a light cotton kimono for summer wear
9	漢字（と）	Chinese characters
	ひらがな	cursive phonetic characters simplified from *kanji* (Chinese characters)
10	本音（と）	one's true feelings or motives
	建前	the face one wears in public

課題

1. 日本事情—英単語—の項目1〜10について3個ずつ英単語を考え、英語と日本語を書きなさい。
2. 日本事情—英文説明—の項目1〜10において2項目を選び、英文を書きなさい。
   2つの事柄を対応させた英文を2セット作成することになります（10行程度×2セット）。
   2つの事柄は日本の中の「並立する」ものになります
   （例：うどんとそば）。

第7章

JAPANESE CULTURE（実践演習）

「第7章 JAPANESE CULTURE（実践演習）」では、日本文化を英文として、実際に紹介していきましょう。さらに、英単語、英文法、英作文の学習も行いましょう。

次の英文を読み理解し、自分の考えを英語で述べてみよう！

I . The Japanese Climate

a. earthquake
b. typhoon

As an island country, Japan faces many climate challenges compared to other countries of the world. Many foreigners think that Japan has one climate, but the truth is that the climate varies all over Japan. Northern Japanese regions, such as Hokkaido, face many snowstorms. On the other hand, southern areas of Japan, such as Okinawa, are more tropical.

Earthquakes, however, are general challenges that Japanese people face everywhere in the country. Multiple times a year, many different cities are at risk from these dangerous natural disasters. Occasionally, earthquakes that take place in the ocean can be followed by a devastating tsunami, but this is a rare occurrence.

Many areas of Japan also suffer from typhoons, which are massive, powerful rain storms. Rather than occurring randomly throughout the year, typhoons usually come during July and August. The regions that are most affected by typhoons are Kyushu and Shikoku, the southern areas of Japan.

From the Western point of view, although Japan suffers from many various natural disasters, the Japanese people seem to respond to the challenges with determination to come together and survive.

WORDS & PHRASES
vary　異なる　　region　地方、地域　　multiple　多数の
disaster　災害、災難　　occasionally　時たま
devastating　破壊的な　　occurrence　出来事
massive　大規模な、大量の　　randomly　でたらめに
respond to 〜　〜に応じる、〜に反応する

a. **Common Questions**
1. What region of Japan has many snowstorms?
2. What natural disaster causes tsunamis?
3. Where do many typhoons take place?
4. During which months do typhoons usually come to Japan?
5. When do earthquakes occur in Japan?

b. **Answers**
1. _____
2. _____
3. _____
   _____

第 7 章 JAPANESE CULTURE（実践演習）

4. _____
   _____
5. _____
   _____

b. **Answers**
1. Northern Japan (Northern Japan has many snowstorms.)
2. Earthquakes (Earthquakes cause tsunamis.)
3. Kyushu and Shikoku (Many typhoons take place in Kyushu and Shikoku.)
4. July and August (Typhoons usually come to Japan during July and August.)
5. Multiple times per year (Earthquakes occur in Japan multiple times a year.

c. **Dialogue Questions**
   ※ F: Foreigner になったつもりで、会話の内容を考えよう。

J: What natural disasters in Japan do you think are the most terrifying?

F: _____
   _____
   _____
   _____

F: Earthquakes are the most terrifying because they are completely unpredictable. Typhoons are much more predictable, and they occur in many other countries, using different names. (Before coming to Japan, I had never experienced an earthquake.)

J: In the United States, which are more dangerous, tornadoes or hurricanes?

F: _____
_____
_____
_____

F: Both cause a lot of damage, but they take place in different locations. More tornadoes occur inland, whereas hurricanes cause the most damage on the coast. Overall, tornadoes cause more deaths on average than hurricanes.

J: What are the climate differences between Japan and the United States?

F: _____
_____
_____
_____
_____
_____

F: The climates are actually rather similar, because they vary so much throughout the countries. The northern regions of both nations face snowstorms, whereas the southern regions are more tropical. They have such similar climates because they lie on the same latitudinal lines. This makes traveling between the two countries much more familiar.

d. 次の英語の（　　）内の語を適切に並べ替えなさい。
1. I think that Japan (suffered, natural, from, compared, more, has, disasters, to) other industrial countries.
2. (The, you, truth, not, blame, is, that, should, others) for your own mistakes.
3. You should throw away (the, order, things, have, that, you, had, in) to get something new.
4. (The, will, computer, that, broke, taken, down, be) to the repair shop tomorrow.
5. People who want to go to America is said to (hard, decreasing, which, in, be, number, to believe, is).

d. 解答欄
1. _____
2. _____
3. _____
4. _____
5. _____

e. 提示された英語を使用し、次の日本語を英語に直しなさい。
1. アメリカの人口と比べると日本の人口は少ない。
   （compared to）

2. 本当のところは日本の国力は弱くなっている。
   (The truth is that)
3. 日本が直面している問題は出生率の下降である。
   (that：関係代名詞の目的格)
4. 子供を産む女性の数は減少している。
   (that：関係代名詞の主格)
5. 日本は新たな方法を考え出す必要があるが、それは簡単ではない。
   (, which)

e. 解答欄
1. _____
2. _____
3. _____
4. _____
5. _____

II. Japanese Religion

a. Shintoism (the hierarchy: the top is the Emperor) 〈positive〉
b. Buddhism (nature) 〈negative〉
c. Christianity (love) 〈fashionable〉
d. temples and shrines

　Japanese religion combines many ideas and traditions within the Japanese society.　The main three religions are Shintoism, Buddhism, and Christianity.　The philosophy of Confucianism also plays a major role in the foundation of the Japanese culture.　They have key

第 7 章 JAPANESE CULTURE（実践演習）

differences in theology and ideas, yet are incorporated in the lives of many Japanese citizens without conflict.

Shintoism, the original religion <u>followed by</u> the indigenous people, emphasizes <u>the belief that</u> all things have spirituality. Many of the positive aspects of the Japanese culture originate from Shinto tradition, such as wedding ceremonies and childbirth celebrations. Since Shintoism was a foundational religion in the Japanese society, the emperor is placed at the top of the hierarchy of Shintoism. Therefore, he is respected as the major symbol of Japan.

Buddhism originated in India, **but it <u>made its way</u> through Asia in the 6th century to become part of the Japanese society as well**. The focus on nature and meditation offered a different way for Japanese people to appreciate the world around them. In modern times, **Buddhist practices <u>account for</u> some of the more negative aspects of life, such as burial ceremonies.**

Finally, Christianity became more popular in Japan after the end of World War II. **<u>As expected,</u> many of the popular Christian traditions in Japan revolve around the fashionable traditions in the West, such as Christmas and St. Valentine's Day.** The ability for these three religions to coexist in the Japanese society shows an aspect of the culture that is unique in the international community.

WORDS & PHRASES
combine　結合する　　philosophy　哲学、原理
Confucianism　儒教　　foundation　基礎、土台
theology　神学　　incorporate　組み入れる　　conflict　争い
indigenous　土着の　　emphasize　強調する
belief　信じること　　tradition　伝統

celebration　祝賀、お祝い　　foundational　基礎となる
emperor　天皇　　hierarchy　階層制度、階層
make one's way　栄える　　focus　焦点　　meditation　瞑想
appreciate　正しく評価する、正しく認識する
account for ～　～を説明する　　burial　埋葬
revolve around　営まれる、展開する　　coexist　共存する

a. Common Questions
1. What is the religion of the indigenous people of Japan?
2. Which Japanese religion originated in India?
3. Which religion became popular after World War II?
4. What philosophy plays a major part in Japanese society?
5. Which Japanese religion has the strongest connection with the emperor?

b. Answers
1. _____
2. _____
3. _____
4. _____
5. _____

b. Answers
1. Shintoism
2. Buddhism
3. Christianity
4. Confucianism
5. Shintoism

第7章 JAPANESE CULTURE (実践演習)

c. Dialogue Questions

※ J: Japanese, F: Foreigner になったつもりで、会話の内容を考えよう。

F: What religion influences you the most and why is that?

J: _____
_____
_____
_____
_____

J: The answer is different for every Japanese person. Often, Japanese families practice Shintoism and Buddhism. They tend to have a Shinto altar in the kitchen and a Buddhist altar in the living room. Additionally, many people celebrate Christmas and St. Valentine's Day with their friends.

J: What religion influences you the most and why is that?

F: _____
_____
_____
_____
_____

F: Likewise, the answer is different for all foreigners. Personally, my family is Catholic, which is a Christian religion. We go to church every Sunday, and all of our major life events, such as birth, wedding, and burial ceremonies are also performed as Catholic ceremonies.

J: Is there more conflict between religions in your country?

F: _____
_____
_____
_____
_____
_____

F: Yes. In my country, it is very uncommon to practice more than one religion. Most families associate with a single faith.
Although it is becoming more common to marry someone from a different religion, it can still be difficult in certain situations. If I married someone who is not Catholic, my family would not be very happy. On the other hand, my other friends can marry people from other religions without difficulty.

d. 次の英語の（　　　）内の語を適切に並べ替えなさい。
1. China has (by, been, great, industrial, achieving, progress, followed) India recently.
2. People should (in, have, the, is, that, there, belief, good) each and every one of us.

3. She (made, lot, way, to, through, a, her, of, hardships) become the CEO of a company.
4. The amount of money (live, for, for, way, an, the, accounts, person, elderly, can) the rest of their life as they wish.
5. She achieved all her goals in life, (knows, expected, as, everybody, by, she).

d. 解答欄
1. _____
2. _____
3. _____
4. _____
5. _____

e. 提示された英語を使用し、次の日本語を英語に直しなさい。
1. 国語は英語の次に好きです。(followed by)
2. 私には夢はかなうという信念があります。(the belief that)
3. 私は信念に従って生きてきました。(make one's way)
4. 私の人生は家族の幸せのために占められています。(account for)
5. 人生は思うようにはなかなかいきません。(as expected)

e. 解答欄
1. _____
2. _____
3. _____
4. _____
5. _____

III. Bushido (The Way of Bushi)

a. Samurai warriors

Bushido, or the way of *bushi* (samurai warriors), <u>refers to</u> the Japanese warrior code of chivalry in the feudal ages. There was a focus on the connection between life and death, **because in the Japanese culture, the idea of death** <u>led</u> *samurai* **warriors** <u>to</u> **understand the value of an honorable life that ends in an honorable death.** In the Edo era, from around the 17th century to the 19th century, the social hierarchy provided political power primarily to *samurai* warriors, followed by farmers, artisans, and merchants, in that order. As a result, commoners should have followed the *samurai* warriors' way of life. **At the time, <u>fewer</u> wars were taking place,** so *samurai* strove to fulfill an honorable life through modest and generous living. Commoners also devoted their life to their work, so that even though they were not warriors, they fulfilled a beautiful life in order to have an honorable death. **This mentality <u>has been maintained</u> in modern times,** so that Japanese citizens feel that it is important to live a modest, generous lifestyle through their hard work. **This <u>makes</u> the continuous improvement of Japanese commodities possible.**

WORDS & PHRASES
warrior　武士、戦士　　code　規約、規定　　chivalry　騎士道
feudal　封建(制度)の　　honorable　尊敬すべき、名誉ある
era　時代　　primarily　第一に

第7章 JAPANESE CULTURE（実践演習）

artisan　職人　　commoner　平民、庶民
take place　起こる　　strive (strove)　努力する
fulfill　遂行する、全うする　　modest　謙虚な、慎み深い
generous　寛大な　　devote　捧げる
mentality　精神性　　maintain　維持する
continuous　継続的な、連続的な　　commodity　商品

a. **Common Questions**
1. What is the Japanese warrior code of chivalry in the feudal ages?
2. What connection in the Japanese culture influenced *Bushido* the most?
3. When was the Edo era?
4. Who was at the top of the social hierarchy in the Edo era?
5. Why were *samurai* able to live an honorable life through modest, generous living during the Edo era?

b. **Answers**
1. _____
2. _____
3. _____
4. _____
5. _____

b. **Answers**
1. *Bushido*, or the way of *bushi*
2. The connection between life and death
3. From the 17th to 19th century
4. *Samurai* warriors

5. At the time, fewer wars were taking place.

c. Dialogue Questions

※ J: Japanese, F: Foreigner になったつもりで、会話の内容を考えよう。

F: Why did the commoners want to follow *Bushido* like the samurai warriors?

J: _____
_____
_____
_____
_____

J: The *samurai* warriors were highly ranked and they taught the commoners' children, so the commoners respected their lifestyle. *Bushido* came to be viewed as a method of understanding life and death that was beneficial to the whole society. Therefore, it was passed down through generations to modern society.

J: How does *Bushido* compare with European chivalry?

F: _____
_____
_____
_____
_____

_____
_____
_____
_____

F: It appears that *Bushido* focuses much more on the existential questions of life and death. Chivalry is primarily focused on the importance of acting like a respectable man in a Christian society. This involves how men should treat women, as well as their role as protectors of their families and lands. Both *Bushido* and chivalry find importance in certain characteristics, such as courage and honor. *Bushido* applies to the entire Japanese society, whereas chivalry only applies to the men of Western society.

F: How does *Bushido* contribute to the improvement of Japanese commodities?

J: _____
_____
_____
_____
_____
_____

J: When the Japanese people work very hard at their individual jobs, they help create products of high quality. They believe that it is important to devote themselves entirely to the job without much concern for the end result. Because of this work ethic, products of high quality are the final results. The Japanese people continue this endeavor in order to live the honorable life that *Bushido* calls for Japanese citizens to follow.

d. 次の英語の（　　　）内の語を適切に並べ替えなさい。
1. When people (to, refer, they, peace, tend, of, think, to) their own.
2. Fear and prejudice may (lead, the, people, world, in, fight, to) against each other.
3. Nowadays (that, fewer, world, people, a, thinking, are, war) may take place compared to before.
4. The Japanese mentality (been, being, modest and hard-working, of, maintained, since, has) the olden times.
5. A strong desire in life will (possible, any, make, dream, you, to, want, accomplish).

d. 解答欄
1. _____
2. _____
3. _____
4. _____
5. _____

e. 提示された英語を使用し、次の日本語を英語に直しなさい。
1. 質問の答えは教科書を参照してください。(refer to)
2. 彼の考えは私に人生の生き方を教えてくれた。
   (lead ～ to understand)

3. 日本ではいじめは少なくなっているとは言えない。（fewer）
4. いじめ問題は昔から日本にはある。（have been maintained）
5. 人口知能は仕事の効率化を可能にしてくれるだろう。
   （make ～ possible）

e. 解答欄
   1. _____
   2. _____
   3. _____
   4. _____
   5. _____

Ⅳ．Promotion According to Age vs. Ability

a. Lifetime employment system
b. *Honne* and *tatemae*

　The Japanese work environment is unique in the international community.　People usually stay in one company for their entire lives. Also, they must follow certain workplace behaviors.
　The lifelong employment system has been in place for many years. It focuses on the idea that promotion is based on seniority.　When you stay with a company for a long time, you are paid more.　In the Japanese workplace, hard work and cooperation tend to be more important than production.　**However, many companies have been changing from this system.**　These companies seem to show interest in the western approach that encourages promotion for individual

production. In western companies, seniority is **less important than in Japanese companies.** This is a dramatic change from the older system, as it provides less security for Japanese workers.

Within the workplace, a specific behavior is expected of all employees. In Japanese, there are two words for expressing personality. The first, *honne*, refers to the true, personal feelings of an individual. This is expected to remain private, and this is inappropriate for the workplace. At work, Japanese employees show *tatemae,* which are their socially accepted opinions that are appropriate for the company. There is another expression, *nemawashi,* which is the practice for Japanese workers to discuss problems before a meeting instead of during a meeting. Disagreements during official meetings are unacceptable. This is a good example of *tatemae.* This way, there can be group harmony in the company. **This is very different from western companies, where workers are expected to give their true feelings during official meetings. Individual feelings are more valued in western companies, so that all ideas are expressed for the benefit of the group.** Final conclusions come from the compromises of employees or the decisions of superiors.

The workplace environment in Japan tends to have specific expectations that ensure a secure, but socially strict, employment.

WORDS & PHRASES
behavior　ふるまい、行動　　in place　機能している
seniority　年功序列　　provide　提供する　　specific　特定の
refer to　～　～に言及する　　inappropriate　不適当な
disagreement　不一致、意見の相違　　official　公式の
value　尊重する　　benefit　利益

compromise　妥協、歩み寄り　　superior　上司
ensure　確実にする、保証する　　secure　安全な
strict　厳しい

a. Common Questions

1. What is important in the lifelong employment system in Japan?
2. What is valued in the western employment system?
3. What is *honne*?
4. What is *tatemae*?
5. What is *nemawashi*?

b. Answers

1. _____
2. _____
3. _____
4. _____
5. _____
   _____

b. Answers

1. Hard work and cooperation
2. Individual production and individual feelings
3. The true feelings of an individual
4. The socially accepted opinions and expressions of an individual
5. The practice for Japanese workers to discuss problems before a meeting instead of during a meeting

c. Dialogue Questions

※ F: Foreigner になったつもりで、会話の内容を考えよう。

J: What do you think of the expectations of the Japanese workplace environment?

F: _____
_____
_____

F: The lifelong employment system gives Japanese workers more security, but it seems to be socially strict because of the use of *tatemae*.

J: How do you think Japanese or western companies should work with foreigners that have different cultures?

F: _____
_____
_____
_____
_____

F: It is important to understand different cultures and why they have different behaviors. It is also important to understand your own culture and why your culture has certain behaviors. This way, when there are disagreements, there will be fewer misunderstandings.

J: Do you think that Japanese employees express *honne* in western companies?

F: _____
_____
_____
_____

F: If a Japanese person is used to western culture, they are more comfortable expressing *honne*. However, if the Japanese employee is not comfortable with the individual culture of the western company, he or she will probably only use *tatemae*.

J: Do you think that foreigners in Japanese companies use only *tatemae*?

F: _____
_____
_____

F: It can be very difficult for a foreigner not to express their *honne* during work. Therefore, it often takes time for the foreigner to adjust to the Japanese *tatemae* culture.

d. 次の英語の（　　）内の語を適切に並べ替えなさい。
1. How (both, in, you, been, have, Tokyo, of, since) your arrival in Japan?

2. The (been, working, due, a, lifestyle, has, changing, lot, to) the advancement of technology in recent years.
3. In order to live a good life, (what, less, do, is, to, important, how, than, to) do it.
4. (Japan, lot, Asian, people, a, have, where, come, of) to work, will surely face problems about how to work with them properly in the near future.
5. People had better utilize AI, (so, working, that, improve, their, they, conditions, can) and outcomes.

d. 解答欄
1. _____
2. _____
3. _____
4. _____
5. _____

e. 提示された英語を使用し、次の日本語を英語に直しなさい。
1. 私はここに3時間ずっといます。(have been)
2. 私は英語を12年間ずっと勉強しています。(have been …ing)
3. 得意なことは好きなことほど重要ではありません。(less important)
4. 私は名古屋に住んでいますが、そこで生まれました。(, where)
5. 私はずっと英語が好きなので、英語が得意になりました。(, so that)

e. 解答欄
1. _____
2. _____
3. _____

4. _____
5. _____

Ⅴ. Japanese Annual Events

a. *Shogatsu*
b. *Hatsumode*
c. *Hinamatsuri*
d. *Hanami*
e. *Koinobori*
f. *Tanabata*
g. *O-bon*
h. *Shichi-go-san*

The annual events of Japan have two main themes that bring Japanese people together in celebration.

The first theme, nature, emphasizes an appreciation for the changing of seasons over time. **There are many examples of this, perhaps the most popular celebration being *Shogatsu*, the celebration of the New Year.** As the year continues, **Japanese people celebrate *Hanami* in the spring, when** cherry trees blossom for a short time. **The brief moment of beauty catches the attention of every eye as flowers fill the streets of multiple cities across the nation.**

The second main theme of major Japanese events is religion. *Hatsumode* is the first religious celebration of the year during *Shogatsu*. Families make their first visit of the new year to a shrine or a temple. **Other** religious events center around the children of

119

Japan. The first, *Hinamatsuri*, is the Doll Festival on March 3rd, which celebrates young girls. Young boys are celebrated at a later festival on May 5th. This festival was originally called "The Boys' Festival", but is now referred to as "Children's Day". *Koinobori*, or streamers designed as carp, are flown at the homes of families around Japan. *Shichi-go-san*, another children's festival, takes place on November 15th. It focuses on the special ages of children from both genders. Seven-year-old girls, five-year-old boys, and three-year-old toddlers all take part in this special day. **Besides the celebration of children, Japanese people also commemorate the spirits of ancestors during *O-bon*, the Buddhist three-day holidays in August, at each region where citizens light lanterns and perform dances.** Most of these annual events originate from Shintoism and Buddhism, the two primary religions of Japan.

The celebration of Japanese annual events is unique in different regions across the nation. However, the importance and excitement around these festivals impact the society as a whole.

第7章 JAPANESE CULTURE（実践演習）

WORDS & PHRASES
theme　主題、テーマ　　emphasize　強調する
appreciation　評価、鑑賞、認識　　over time　時間を超えて、ずっと
blossom　開花する　　brief　短時間の　　multiple　多数の
streamer　吹き流し、流れるもの　　flow (- flew - flown)　流す
gender　性別　　toddler　よちよち歩く人、歩き始めの子供
besides　～　～の他にも、～に加えて　　commemorate　記念する、祝う
ancestor　先祖　　lantern　手さげランプ、提灯　　primary　主要な

a. Common Questions
1. What are the two main themes of Japanese festivals?
2. What is the festival that celebrates cherry blossoms in the spring?
3. What was the original name for "Children's Day"?
4. What is the festival that celebrates the special ages of children from both genders?
5. From which Japanese religion does *O-bon* originate?

b. Answers
1. _____
2. _____
3. _____
4. _____
5. _____

b. Answers
1. Nature and religion
2. *Hanami*

3. The Boys' Festival
4. *Shichi-go-san*
5. Buddhism

c. Dialogue Questions

※ F: Foreigner になったつもりで、会話の内容を考えよう。

J: What are the main themes for most of the annual events in America?

F: _____
_____
_____
_____
_____

F: The two main themes for American holidays are politics and religion. For example, the Fourth of July is a major holiday that celebrates American independence in 1776. In addition to this, Thanksgiving Day originated from the communication between the Native Americans and the American settlers.

J: What about the religious holidays?

F: _____
_____
_____
_____

_____

_____

F: There are many religious holidays celebrated in the United States, and most of them are originally Christian holidays. However, even citizens who are not Christian still celebrate many of them. For example, St. Valentine's Day, Easter, and Christmas are all originally Christian holidays, but they are popular throughout American culture.

J: Why do you think Japanese holidays focus on nature while American holidays focus on politics?

F: _____

_____

_____

_____

_____

_____

F: Japan has been shaped and influenced by nature, whether positive or negative, since the origin of the nation. Therefore, the Japanese people place more emphasis on the nature that has always held a major influence on their lives. On the other hand, since American culture is focused on the political freedoms that attract immigrants from many different cultures, the political history is an important aspect of annual celebrations.

d. 次の英語の（　　　）内の語を適切に並べ替えなさい。

1. This (the, will, I, matter, case, support, being, you, no) what people say about you.
2. In (when, many, from, the, people, over, all, 2020, world) will come to Tokyo, it may be a wonderful chance for Japan to show the greatness of her culture.
3. Not only from our successes (but, our, as, failures, from, we, learn, can, more) we grow older.
4. Some students are obedient to their teachers, but (not, students, do, always, follow, other) suit.
5. Tokyo (top, is, the, where, many, place, cultural), industrial and scientific brains from across the world come together.

d. 解答欄
1. _____
2. _____
3. _____
4. _____
5. _____

e. 提示された英語を使用し、次の日本語を英語に直しなさい。

1. その製品は品質が良いようだが、その評価は正しい。(being)
2. 先週の日曜日の午後花見に行ったが、その時は人が一杯だった。(, when)
3. 花が散るごとに、悲しくなる。(as)
4. 花が散って悲しくなる人もいれば、何も感じない人もいる。(other)
5. 日本では正月は離れている家族が再び集まる最大の行事である。(where)

e. 解答欄
1. _____
2. _____
3. _____
4. _____
5. _____

VI. Japanese Tourism

1. Mt. Fuji
2. The Shinkansen
3. Ryokan
4. Kyoto
5. Nara (The Great Buddha of Nara)

Japan attracts many tourists through unique, native traditions. From the iconic image of Mt. Fuji outside of Tokyo to the image of the Great Buddha located in Nara, there are many specific destinations that draw crowds from all over the world. **These places are made accessible through the Japanese transportation system, primarily through the Shinkansen, the bullet train.**

The incredibly fast Shinkansen <u>makes it possible for</u> travelers <u>to</u> access Japan all the way from Kyushu, the southernmost point, to Hokkaido, the northernmost island of the country. <u>While traveling</u> between these two points, one can visit various cities along the way. Each has its own individual traditions and attractions.

Kyoto is probably one of the most famous destinations for domestic and international travelers alike. The old city is the previous capital of Japan, although it is very different from the current capital, Tokyo. **This allows tourists to experience both the traditional and modern aspects of the nation.**

   During their travels, many tourists choose to stay in the traditional Japanese ryokan located all over Japan, primarily in older cities. **These places let tourists sleep on Japanese tatami mats and eat traditional Japanese meals.** These main attractions demonstrate the Japanese culture that interests international tourists.

WORDS & PHRASES
attract　引きつける、魅惑する　　native　自国の
iconic　類型的な　　destination　目的地
accessible　接近できる、近づきやすい　　primarily　主として
alike　同様に　　current　現在の
demonstrate　説明する、実際にやって見せる

a. Common Questions
1. Where is the statue of the Great Buddha located?
2. What is the Japanese name of the bullet train?
3. What is the northernmost island of Japan?
4. What is the previous capital of Japan?
5. Where do people sleep in Japanese ryokan?

b. Answers
1. _____
2. _____
3. _____

第 7 章 JAPANESE CULTURE（実践演習）

4. _____
5. _____

b. Answers

1. Nara
2. The Shinkansen
3. Hokkaido
4. Kyoto
5. *Tatami* (mats)

c. Dialogue Questions

※ F: Foreigner になったつもりで、会話の内容を考えよう。

J: Where was your favorite place to travel in Japan and why was that?

F: _____
_____
_____
_____
_____
_____
_____
_____

F: I was able to travel to Miyajima in the Hiroshima prefecture with my family, and that was my favorite city so far. I loved the iconic,

127

beautiful shrine at sea surrounded by nature on its own peaceful island. There were many tourists, but it was easy to find peace and quiet by taking a nice hike along the mountainous paths. There were even more deer than tourists around the shrine, which was interesting because deer are supposed to be the messengers of gods. Also, the famous momiji cakes were delicious omiyage, or souvenirs.

J: What do you think are the key words for Japanese culture?

F: _____
_____
_____
_____
_____
_____

F: The Japanese culture is an interesting mixture of traditionalism and modernism. For example, Kyoto is a very traditional city, with many temples and shrines, even though it is a busy, economic city. Tokyo, on the other hand, is a modern metropolis, but even Tokyo has famous older temples that are easily accessible.

J: What do you think are the key words for American culture?

F: _____
_____
_____

F: American culture is primarily focused on freedom and cultural integration. The American society is built from multiple different cultures around the world, so it is referred to as a melting pot. These people are attracted to the idea of the various freedoms that America offers, such as freedom of speech, religion, the press, along with others. Most American celebrations and monuments are dedicated to the work that has progressed freedom and cultural integration.

d. 次の英語の（　　）内の語を適切に並べ替えなさい。
1. These experiences (own, made, you, possible, are, on, when, travel, more, your) than when you do in a group.
2. The incredibly unique experience makes (for, travel, us, high, again, possible, to, with, it, the) motivation of studying English harder.
3. While (Europe, we, from, can, various, to, people, traveling, meet) different countries through the trip.
4. This allows (but, to, not, about, about, know, foreign, only, us, cultures) our own culture.
5. These (grow, experiences, just, mentally, than, you, let, you, more) live inside Japan.

d. 解答欄
1. _____
2. _____
3. _____
4. _____
5. _____

e. 提示された英語を使用し、次の日本語を英語に直しなさい。
1. 海外旅行をしている間、多くの人々にあった。(while traveling)
2. 旅行は私達に様々な人と会うことを可能にしてくれる。(allow 〜 to)
3. 旅行は新しい自分との出会いを可能にしてくれる。(let 〜)
4. 一人で旅行をすると、私達に未知の事柄を経験させてくれる。(make it possible for 〜 to)
5. 未知の事柄を経験することは、一人で旅行することによって可能になる。(made possible)

e. 解答欄
1. _____
2. _____
3. _____
4. _____
5. _____

あとがき

　長年、英語教育、英語学、通訳ガイドなど英語に関する学習指導を行ってきた筆者は、適切なテキストがなく苦労してきました。そこで、学習指導をまとめて、それを学習者に提示したいという大きな希望を持っていました。今回、この希望を実現させることができ、学習者の勉強に役立てることができるようになったことに感謝し、学習者が本書を利用し、英語に関する造詣をさらに深めることができることを祈っております。

　本書が成立する上で、愛知産業大学の学生である片瀬このみさん、光崎朱音さん、長谷川航大さん、ふくろう出版の亀山裕幸氏ほか、多くの人々のご協力をいただきました。この場をお借りして謝意を表したいと思います。大変ありがとうございます。

　本書をきっかけとし、多くの人々が英語に、より一層興味を抱いてもらえるようになれば、筆者の望外の喜びです。

執筆者略歴

西田一弘　愛知産業大学短期大学国際コミュニケーション学科准教授、（株）兼松江商勤務、関西学院大学商学部卒業、愛知淑徳大学大学院コミュニケーション研究科異文化コミュニケーション専攻　博士前期課程修了、博士課程後期課程単位取得満期退学、東京大学大学院総合文化研究科言語情報科学専攻　修士課程単位取得満期退学、名古屋大学大学院人文学研究科人文学専攻言語学専門　博士課程前期課程修了、博士課程後期課程単位取得満期退学

JCOPY 〈(社)出版者著作権管理機構 委託出版物〉
本書の無断複写（電子化を含む）は著作権法上での例外を除き禁じられています。本書をコピーされる場合は、そのつど事前に(社)出版者著作権管理機構（電話 03-5244-5088、FAX 03-5244-5089、e-mail: info@jcopy.or.jp）の許諾を得てください。
また本書を代行業者等の第三者に依頼してスキャンやデジタル化することは、たとえ個人や家庭内での利用であっても著作権法上認められておりません。

英語通訳ガイドの基礎知識

2025 年 4 月 8 日　初版発行

著　者　　西田　一弘

発　行　　**ふくろう出版**

〒700-0035　岡山市北区高柳西町 1-23
　　　　　　友野印刷ビル
TEL：086-255-2181
FAX：086-255-6324
http://www.296.jp
e-mail：info@296.jp
振替　01310-8-95147

印刷・製本　　友野印刷株式会社
ISBN978-4-86186-934-1 C3082
©NISHIDA Kazuhiro 2025

定価はカバーに表示してあります。乱丁・落丁はお取り替えいたします。